# BEYOND
# CHARLES
# AND DIANA

By the same authors

*Beyond Jennifer & Jason: An Enlightened Guide to Naming Your Baby*

*Beyond Sarah & Sam: An Enlightened Guide to Jewish Baby Naming*

*Beyond Shannon & Sean: An Enlightened Guide to Irish Baby Naming*

# BEYOND CHARLES AND DIANA

## AN ANGLOPHILE'S GUIDE TO BABY NAMING

• • • • • • • • • • • • • •

LINDA ROSENKRANTZ
& PAMELA REDMOND SATRAN

**St. Martin's Press
New York**

Library of Congress Cataloging-in-Publication Data

Rosenkrantz, Linda.
        Beyond Charles & Diana : an anglophile's guide to baby naming /
Linda Rosenkrantz and Pamela Redmond Satran.
                p.  cm.
        Includes index.
        ISBN 0-312-06901-4 — ISBN 0-312-06902-2 (pbk.)
        1. Names, Personal—United States.   2. Names, Personal—English.
I. Satran, Pamela Redmond.   II. Title.   III. Title: Beyond Charles
and Diana.
CS2377.R665   1992
929.4'0892—dc20                                                91-41649
                                                                   CIP

First Edition: March 1992

10 9 8 7 6 5 4 3 2 1

# CONTENTS

# ACKNOWLEDGMENTS

Our thanks go to our editor at St. Martin's, Hope Dellon, for her unfailing support and perceptive input, and to Abigail Kamen for many valuable suggestions, as well as to our equally supportive agent, Molly Friedrich. Our appreciation, too, for special kindnesses to Ami Stilwell, Paul and Ann Babb, Lisa Vaughn, Jenny Walden, Gwyneth and Towyn Mason, Alexander Collins, Michael Suissa, and Beatrice Finch. And finally thanks, as always, to our husbands, Christopher Finch and Richard Satran, for continuing to understand the obsession, and to our wonderful children, Chloe Finch, Rory Satran, and Joe Satran.

# INTRODUCTION

You stayed up till 2 A.M. reading *Jane Eyre*. You woke up at 4 A.M. to watch the royal wedding. And like the rest of the world, you waited with bated breath to hear the names of Britain's newborn princes and princesses.

But unlike the rest of the world, you didn't snicker at Henry or Beatrice or even Eugenie. Those sorts of English names that seem at once familiar and exotic—Cressida and Trevor and Arabella and Alistair—have always fascinated you. Instead of wondering how Charles and Diana and Andy and Fergie could have chosen such offbeat names for their children, you wondered where you could find more just like them.

Here's where. *Beyond Charles & Diana* is the name book for American parents who see Camilla as more appealing than Kayla, who find James more tasteful than Jason, who view British names like Hugo and Harriet and Oliver and Olivia as charmingly eccentric rather than just plain weird. And what you'll find here is not only the entire empire of British names—from stalwarts like Elizabeth and Philip or Charles and Diana to quirky characters like Poppy and Piers—but also a context for understanding them.

*Beyond Charles & Diana* continues the format that has made our original name book, *Beyond Jennifer & Jason*, so popular. Rather than offering one long alphabetical list of names, we categorize names according to the interests and concerns of modern parents: where names stand in terms of class, for instance, which names are fashionable in England, which names have been favored by the royals, and which names are found only in Britain. These are organized into seven major sections:

*British Style:* What's hot, what's hip, and what's not in England right now, as well as how British naming style compares with that in America. Also, names fashionable in England that may sound a fresh note to American parents' ears as well as what British stars are naming their babies.

*The Royals:* A complete catalog of royal names, from Ethelred to Eugenie, plus a compendium of Scottish royal names. Did you know there really was a King Macbeth? And that if Queen Victoria had gotten her way, there would now be only one royal male name today: Albert? Here, thankfully, are dozens of other tradition-honored options.

*Class Consciousness:* Which names are "U" (upper class), which names aren't, how they got that way, and why you should (or shouldn't) care.

*Literary Lights:* A cast of British characters—from Shakespeare to Dickens, from Jane Austen to Barbara Pym—sure to provide naming inspiration for the literary-minded parent.

*There'll Always Be an England:* There are some things—Harrods, high tea, and the name Harriet, for instance—that can be considered quintessentially British. In this section are names that are familiar here but that get quite different accents there, as well as names confined almost exclusively to Britain. Just as they say "jumper," "lift," and "loo," they name their children Primrose and Jessamine and Jasper. Plus dozens of other fresh choices for the American parent in search of an unusual name.

*Scottish Names:* Names particularly popular in Scotland—Fiona, Georgina, Angus, Duncan, and clan names—as well as those peculiar to it: Bethia, Ishbel, Hamish, or Mungo, anyone?

*Welsh Names:* For the parent looking for a name that's truly off the beaten track, a wide assortment from this beautiful corner of Britain.

You'll find many of the names in this book as familiar as Princess Diana's smile, while many others will seem as novel—and, we hope, refreshing—as a hike through the Moors or a pint of Ruddles County ale. Likewise, you may find many of the names here friendly to your precinct of America, while others may seem—like steak and kidney pie or stewed eel—best left to the English. Where you draw the line, and on which side of it you choose to stand, is up to you. What you'll get from this book is the complete complement of British names, and in the end, the pleasure of knowing you've made a thoughtful and enlightened choice, whether you decide to move beyond Charles and Diana or not.

# BRITISH STYLE

The style of names in Britain has always been similar to American style, with a few fairly radical differences. In some instances we follow their path, in others they pick up on ours, and, quite often, we just happen to like the same names at the same time. At the moment, for instance, both British and American parents are naming their children Jessica, Emily, Alexandra, Alexander, William, and Samuel in great numbers. In 1950, parents on both sides of the Atlantic favored Linda, Susan, and Patricia for girls, Michael, John, and David for boys.

Style in names is like style in anything else, and much of it is transatlantic. In 1991, in addition to naming their children Jessica and Sam, both British and American couples bought Madonna records, watched "Cheers" and "Twin Peaks," and wore jeans bought at The Gap. But hip parents in Hampstead also bought baby clothes at Trotters and parenting books by Paula Yates, wife of Live Aid organizer Bob Geldof.

So too did they name their daughters Charlotte, Alice, Sophie, and Georgina and their sons Oliver, Henry, and George with much greater frequency than their American peers, who favored instead such names as Ashley, Brittany, Kayla, Joshua, and Kyle—all nearly unheard of in the UK— not to mention Justin, which was already on the British popularity polls fifteen years ago.

More adventurous British parents plumbed areas left dormant by Americans: London pushchairs ("strollers" to you) are filled these days with rosy-cheeked little Helens and Hugos and Clementines and Felixes, while those names have not penetrated even the innermost circles of New York or L.A.

In general, British style favors the extremes: the strictly traditional, especially for boys, as well as the most eccentric, primarily for girls. Picture a tweed hacking jacket worn with purple suede ankle boots, a proper black dress with chandelier earrings, black tie combined with a kilt. Time-honored royal names—Anne, Elizabeth, Victoria, Charles, William, James, Henry—mix comfortably with the offbeat and the exotic: Poppy, Primrose, Iona, Cressida, Basil, Archie, and Piers.

The result is a fusion of formality and charm that is quintessentially English: a language of names that is at once familiar and foreign, a language that Americans can, if they choose, rightfully call their own.

# WHAT'S HOT

If you want to know what names are fashionable, more than one hip British parent has said, read the birth announcements in *The Independent*, London's yuppie newspaper. The scoop is that traditionally minded parents tend to announce young Charlotte's or Charles's arrival in *The Times*, while more stylish mums and dads opt to advertise Harriet's or Hugo's (and Hugo, by the way, is absolutely the hottest name in England) birth in *The Independent*.

Wait a minute: Hugo? Is British naming style really that divergent from America's? Well, yes and no. There are some marked similarities: British parents, for instance, share their American counterparts' renewed appreciation of very traditional names like Catherine and Peter and Daniel and Anna. And names that combine an old-fashioned, almost musty quality with a certain irreverence for conventional taste— Eleanor and Madeleine and Hugh—are the height of fashion on both sides of the Atlantic.

But while Eleanor and Hugh mark the outer boundaries of

how far most stylish American parents will go when choosing a classic-yet-quirky name, Britons are striking out more adventurously into this territory. Clementine (pronounced *Clementeen*), Iona, Josephine, Florence, Archie, Felix, and, yes, Hugo are almost unheard of in the United States, yet they're distinctly fashionable and increasingly used by English parents. Even some of the more solidly traditional names being revived by British parents—Richard, for example, and Helen and Ruth—are still in mothballs in America.

Of course, there are names that are fashionable in the United States that are likewise ignored in England. British parents do not, as a rule, give surnames as first names to their children, male or female. There are few if any little Jordans, Morgans, Lanes, or Lowells running around English playgrounds. And while some of the grandma and grandpa names so stylish in the U.S.—notably Sam, Max, Harry, Jack, Anna, Emma, Hannah, Lily, and Sophie—also make a fashion statement in London, others—Jake and Sadie, for instance—have no relevance in Britain. Why? Probably because they're too ethnic, i.e., Irish or Jewish, for this nation of original WASPs, whose grandmothers and grandfathers were named Camilla or Harriet or Frederick or even Hugo.

Here, gleaned from 1990 birth announcements both in *The Independent* and *The London Times,* as well as from nursery-school rosters and playgrounds in the trendier parts of London, are names that are fashionable in Britain right now:

## G I R L S

| | |
|---|---|
| AMELIA | ANNABEL |
| ANASTASIA | BEATRIX |
| ANNA | CAMILLA |

CATHERINE (this is
now the stylish
spelling)
CLARE (more
fashionable than
Claire)
CLAUDIA
CLEMENCY
CLEMENTINE
ELEANOR
ELLA
EMMA
FELICITY
FLORA
FLORENCE
FRANCESCA
HANNAH
HARRIET
HELEN

HELENA
HOLLY
IONA
IONE
ISABEL
JOANNA
JOSEPHINE
JULIET
KATERINA/KATRINA
LAURA
LOUISE
MADELEINE
MAY
MILLICENT
MIRANDA
NATASHA
PHOEBE
ROSE
RUTH

## B O Y S

ALASDAIR
ARCHIE
AUGUSTINE
BASIL
BENEDICT
DANIEL
DOMINIC
EDMUND
FELIX

FREDERICK
HARRY
HUGH
HUGO
JACK
LEO
LOUIS
LUCAS
LUCIEN

LUKE
MALCOLM
MARTIN
MAX
MAXWELL
NICHOLAS
OSCAR

PETER
PIERS
RICHARD
ROLAND
TIMOTHY
TOBIAS
TOBY

# THE BRIT HIT PARADE

In England, unlike America, there is a nationwide newspaper of record, so the birth announcements recorded therein give a pretty good indication of the most popular names in the realm. The following is the 1990 baby name list for *The London Times,* and in parenthesis, where applicable, the relative position of those names that appeared on the comparable American list.

You'll note that the top girl's name on the British list is one that is just beginning to resurface in America after a long nap, and only two of the British girls' names were among the top twenty-five in the U.S. Jessica, in the number one or two position in America for several years, was favored across the Big Pond for the first time, whereas the most popular boy's name in the U.S., Michael, was nowhere to be seen in Blighty. In fact, the British male list has a strong Royalist flavor— seven of the ten leaders are names of past sovereigns.

### G I R L S

1. CHARLOTTE
2. SOPHIE
3. LUCY
4. EMILY (#16 in the U.S.)
5. ALEXANDRA
6. ALICE
7. EMMA
8. JESSICA (2)
9. OLIVIA
10. GEORGINA

### B O Y S

1. JAMES (#9 in the U.S.)
2. THOMAS
3. ALEXANDER
4. WILLIAM (19)
5. OLIVER
6. CHARLES (25)
7. EDWARD
8. GEORGE
9. HENRY
10. SAMUEL

In Britain, considerably more attention is paid to middle names, and it is not unusual for a baby to be presented, like the royals, with not one or two but three of them. Following are the 1990 lists for most popular names used anywhere from first to fourth place:

### G I R L S

1. ELIZABETH (#10 in the U.S.)
2. CHARLOTTE
3. ALICE
4. ALEXANDRA
5. SOPHIE
6. LUCY
7. EMILY (16)
8. VICTORIA
9. KATHERINE
10. EMMA

## B O Y S

1. JAMES (for the twenty-seventh consecutive year; #9 in the U.S.)
2. WILLIAM (19)
3. ALEXANDER
4. THOMAS
5. JOHN (14)
6. EDWARD
7. CHARLES (25)
8. GEORGE
9. DAVID (7)
10. HENRY

# BRIT STARBABIES

If the British have a predilection for eccentric names, and stars have a similar leaning toward the offbeat, then it follows that British stars would choose the quirkiest names of all for their children. This theory is indeed borne out by fact, as evidenced by the following list of names of children of British celebrities. Sure, there are the normal Seans and Elizabeths and Jameses—and even, in the case of Jeremy Irons, the ultratrendy Sam and Max—but these are more than offset by names that range from the unusual to the bizarre.

Sting, for instance, has a baby daughter named Eliot. Peter O'Toole's son is named Lorcan. The three young daughters of rocker Bob Geldof are Fifi Trixiebelle, Peaches, and Little Pixie. And David Bowie has the now nearly grown Zowie, whose infamously strange name perhaps inspired the junior generation of Tyrones and Theodoras.

Here, then, what British stars have been naming their children:

ACE (boy) . . . . . . . . . . Hayley Mills and Leigh Lawson
ADAM . . . . . . . . . . . . . Maurice Gibb
AIMEE . . . . . . . . . . . . . Ozzy Osborne
ALEXANDRIA . . . . . . Keith Richards and Patti Hanson
AMBER ROSE . . . . . . . Yasmin and Simon LeBon
ANNABEL . . . . . . . . . . Lynn Redgrave
ASHLEY (girl) . . . . . . . Barry Gibb
BRIGITTE MICHAEL . Sting
CARLY (girl) . . . . . . . . Twiggy
CHARLIE . . . . . . . . . . . Malcolm McDowell and Mary Steen-
burgen
CRISPIAN . . . . . . . . . . Hayley Mills and Roy Boulting
DHANI (boy) . . . . . . . . George Harrison
ELIOT PAULINE (girl)  Sting
ELIZABETH
SCARLETT . . . . . . . . . Mick Jagger and Jerry Hall
FIFI TRIXIEBELLE . . . Bob Geldof and Paula Yates
IMOGEN . . . . . . . . . . . Andrew Lloyd Weber
JACK . . . . . . . . . . . . . . . Ozzy Osborne
JAKE . . . . . . . . . . . . . . . Sting
JAMES . . . . . . . . . . . . . Robert Palmer
JAMES LEROY
AUGUSTIN . . . . . . . . . Mick Jagger and Jerry Hall
JAMES PAUL . . . . . . . Paul and Linda McCartney
JANE . . . . . . . . . . . . . . . Robert Palmer
JOE . . . . . . . . . . . . . . . . Sting
JOHN ALBERT
VICTOR . . . . . . . . . . . Tracey Ullman
KATE . . . . . . . . . . . . . . Sting
KATHARINE . . . . . . . . Jane Seymour
KELLY (girl) . . . . . . . . Ozzy Osborne
KIMBERLY . . . . . . . . . Rod Stewart and Alana Hamilton
LILLIE . . . . . . . . . . . . . Phil Collins
LILLIE . . . . . . . . . . . . . Malcolm McDowell and Mary Steen-
burgen
LITTLE PIXIE . . . . . . . Bob Geldof and Paula Yates
LOGAN ROMERO . . . Robert Plant

LORCAN . . . . . . . . . . Peter O'Toole
MABLE ELLEN . . . . . . Tracey Ullman
MATILDA . . . . . . . . . . Rachel Ward and Bryan Brown
MAXIMILIAN PAUL . Jeremy Irons and Sinead Cusack
MICHAEL . . . . . . . . . . Barry Gibb
NATALIE . . . . . . . . . . Chrissie Hynde
NATASHA . . . . . . . . . Michael Caine
NICHOLAS . . . . . . . . Andrew Lloyd Weber
OLIVER . . . . . . . . . . . . Amanda Pays and Corbin Bernsen
ORLANDO . . . . . . . . Susannah York
PATRICK . . . . . . . . . . Dudley Moore and Tuesday Weld
PEACHES . . . . . . . . . . Bob Geldof and Paula Yates
PETA (girl) . . . . . . . . . Andy Gibb
ROSIE . . . . . . . . . . . . . Rachel Ward and Bryan Brown
ROSIE LEA . . . . . . . . Roger Daltry
RUBY . . . . . . . . . . . . . Rod Stewart and Kelly Emberg
SAFFRON . . . . . . . . . Simon and Yasmin LeBon
SAMANTHA . . . . . . . . Maurice Gibb
SAMUEL JAMES . . . . Jeremy Irons and Sinead Cusack
SASHA (girl) . . . . . . . Susannah York
SEAN . . . . . . . . . . . . . Jane Seymour
SEAN RODERICK . . . Rod Stewart and Alana Hamilton
STELLA . . . . . . . . . . . . Paul and Linda McCartney
THEODORA DUPREE Keith Richards and Patti Hanson
TRAVIS . . . . . . . . . . . . Barry Gibb
TYRONE . . . . . . . . . . Ron Wood
TYSON (girl) . . . . . . . Nenah Cherry
VASILE (boy) . . . . . . . George Harrison
WILLEM WOLFE . . . . Billy Idol
WILLOW AMBER . . . . Roger Daltry
YASMIN . . . . . . . . . . . Chrissie Hynde
ZOWIE (boy)* . . . . . . . David Bowie

*Who has dropped that name in favor of Joey.

# THE BRYLCREEM
# BOYS

---

There is a jaunty group of names we associate with the dashing World War II RAF pilots, who were sometimes referred to as the Brylcreem Boys. These names are on the cutting edge of fashion, combining the white-silk–scarved style of upper-crust England with the élan of the leather bomber jacket. Some names in this category have already crossed the Atlantic—Ian, Derek, Oliver, and Trevor, for example—but here are some others you might like to consider:

| | |
|---|---|
| ADRIAN | DUNCAN |
| ALISTAIR | GILES |
| BASIL | GRAHAM |
| CLIVE | GUY |
| COLIN | HUGH |
| CRISPIN | IVOR |
| DAMIAN | JULIAN |
| DESMOND | LESLIE |

| | |
|---|---|
| LIONEL | ROBIN |
| MALCOLM | ROLF |
| MILES | ROLLIN |
| NEVILLE | ROLLO |
| NIGEL | RUPERT |
| NOEL | SEBASTIAN |
| REX | TARQUIN |

# Names botanica

While Americans have been known to tiptoe through the tulips—a Lily here, a Rose there, a Daisy there—the nomenclature of the Brits, the gardening fanatics of the world, is a virtual hothouse of names in full bloom. (And these names are *really* used!)

> She did not like to be reminded that she had been christened Violet, from some confused Wordsworthian fancy of her father's—'a violet by a mossy stone, half hidden from the eye'—such a charming idea, he had thought, not realizing that the name Violet did not really suggest this. When she was seventeen she had called herself Viola.
>
> —Barbara Pym, *No Fond Return of Love*

AMARYLLIS
ANEMONE
ANGELICA
AZALEA
CAMELLIA
CHRYSANTHEMUM
CLOVE
CLOVER
DAFFODIL
DAHLIA·
FERN
FLEUR
FLORA
HEATHER
HOLLY
HYACINTH
IRIS
IVY
JASMINE

JONQUIL
LAUREL
LILAC
MAGNOLIA
MARGUERITE
MARIGOLD
MYRTLE
NARCISSUS
PANSY
PEONY
PETUNIA
POPPY
POSY
PRIMROSE
SAFFRON
TANSY
VIOLET
ZINNIA

# Why can't a woman be more like a man?

There is a much stronger tradition in the UK than in the U.S. for the use of feminized masculine names. Of course there are plenty of American Stephanies, Samanthas, and Danielles, but there are far more feminizations that have been popular in England for years and yet are infrequently used on our side of the Big Pond. Among them are:

| | |
|---|---|
| ALBERTINE | CLEMENTINE |
| ANTONIA | CORNELIA |
| AUGUSTA | DAVIDA |
| BERNADETTE | DOMENICA |
| BERNARDINE | EDWINA |
| BRIANA | ERNESTINE |
| BRYONY | EUGENIA/EUGENIE |
| CECILIA | FREDERICA |
| CECILY | GEORGIA |
| CHRISTABEL | GEORGIANA |

| | |
|---|---|
| GEORGINA | PAULINE |
| JACOBA | PETA |
| JACQUETTA | PHILIPPA |
| JOSEPHA | PIPPA |
| JUSTINA | RICHARDA |
| MICHAELA | ROBINA |
| NICOLA/NICOLETTE | RODERICA |
| OCTAVIA | THEODORA |
| OTTALIE/OTTOLINE | THOMASA |

In addition, several of the names that are zooming back to popularity in aristo-Britain after a hundred-year hiatus are offshoots of male names. These include:

| | |
|---|---|
| CHARLOTTE | JOSEPHINE |
| GERALDINE | LOUISE |
| HARRIET | NATALIE |
| HENRIETTA | |

---

'You say your name is George?'

'Yes, sir.'

'Then my eldest child shall be christened George. Or, if female, Georgina.'

'Thank you very much, sir.'

'Not at all,' said Brancepeth. 'A pleasure.'

—P. G. Wodehouse, *Lord Emsworth and Others*

# EXOTICA

The British aristocracy, intelligentsia, and artistic and literary crowds have long had an affinity for exotic names for girls. Some of these—Maria, Sophia, and Anna, for instance—have become as common in Britain as shepherd's pie. Others still sound incongruously Latin or otherwise "foreign" to the untrained ear. But rest assured, there's no name more idiosyncratically English than an exotic first name—Francesca, Natasha, Melita—paired with a thoroughly British surname like Brown or Windsor.

Why this penchant for exotica? Well, Britain is, after all, part of Europe, and many British parents like to show off their Continental sophistication by giving their daughters Italian or Greek or French names. Upper-class and artistic-leaning Brits have traditionally made a post-university sortie to, typically, Italy, and the aristocracy retain their eighteenth-century forebears' passion for things Italianate. Some exotic names are even literal place names, often with a romantic and personal association: Lord and Lady Brocket, for instance, named their daughter Antalya after the Turkish coastal town where they were stranded when Lady B was pregnant.

Exotic names in favor also include those with a mythological reference: Jocasta, Pandora, Olympia, for example. And the British tradition of eccentricity, evidenced by the offbeat or even unique names included here, accounts for much of the English preference for exotic names.

Those of us with non-British surnames often have difficulty pulling off names of mixed ethnicity: pairings like Bridget Kowalski, Kirsten Fanucci, and Luciana Greenberg often sound just plain silly. So how do the British get away with it? Maybe it's because they do it so consistently that names like Gabriella Smith-Jones or Natania Hamilton no longer sound odd to the British themselves. Or maybe they get away with it the same way they get away with wearing Mad Hatter confections on their heads, showing darts and snooker on TV every night, and exalting the royal family despite its obsolescence: by indulging both whims and traditions without caring what the rest of the world thinks.

Here, a selection of British exotica, commonplace as well as unusual:

| | |
|---|---|
| ALLEGRA | CANDIDA |
| ANASTASIA | CARINA |
| ANGELICA | CARINTHIA |
| ANTALYA | CHIARA |
| ANTHEA | CHINA |
| ANTONIA | CHLOE |
| APPOLLONIA | CLEO |
| ARABELLA | COCO |
| AURELIA | CONSUELO |
| AURORA | COSIMA |

CRESSIDA
DAVINA
DELPHINA
DEMETRA
DIANTHA
DREA
EMERALD
FLAVIA
FRANCESCA
GABRIELLA
INDIA
INDRE
ISABELLA
ITHACA
JADE
JOCASTA ✓
LUCIA
MARCA
MARIELLA
MARIS(S)A
MELANTHA
MELITA
MERCEDES
MIRABEL
NATALYA
NATANIA
NATASHA
OCTAVIA
ODESSA
OLYMPIA
OPHELIA

ORIANA
PALOMA
PANDORA
PERDITA
PETRA
PETRONILLA
PILAR
PORTIA
RAFFAELA
RAMONA
ROMANA
ROMILLY
ROMY
SABRINA
SAFFRON
SELENA
SERAPHINA
SERENA
SIENA
SIMONETTA
SYLVIE
TABITHA
TAMARA
TAMSIN
TANIA
TAVIA
VALENTINA
VENETIA
VERENA
YASMINE

# LONDON LIMBO

In Britain, as in the United States, there is a whole contingent of names dangling in fashion limbo. These include Vera Lynn–WW II–home front names and sixties dollybird names. In other words, names that have been, for the most part, overused by parents in recently past decades. They are too dated to be in style, but that doesn't necessarily mean they're out forever. In this category are:

## GIRLS

| | |
|---|---|
| ALMA | BARBARA |
| ANGELA | BERYL |
| ANITA | BETTY |
| ARLENE | BEVERLY |
| AUDREY | BRENDA |
| AVRIL | CAROL |

CYNTHIA
DAPHNE
DAWN
DEIRDRE
DENISE
DIANE
DONNA
DOREEN
DORIS
DOROTHY
EDITH
EILEEN
ELAINE
ENID
ETHEL
EUNICE
IRENE
IRIS
JANET
JANICE
JEAN
JOAN
JOANNE
JOYCE
KELLY
KIM
LILIAN

LINDA
LISA
LUCILLE
LYNN
LYNSEY
MARJORIE
MAUREEN
MICHELLE
MURIEL
NANCY
NOREEN
PATRICIA
PHYLLIS
RHODA
RITA
SANDRA
SHARON
SHEILA
SHIRLEY
SIBYL
SUSAN
SYLVIA
TRACY
VERA
VIVIAN
WENDY
YVONNE

## B O Y S

ALAN
ALBERT
ALFRED
BARRY
BERNARD
BRIAN
DARREN
DENNIS
DONALD
ERIC
ERNEST
GEOFFREY
GERALD
GILBERT
HAROLD
HERBERT
HOWARD
JAMIE
KEITH
KENNETH

KEVIN
LAWRENCE
LEONARD
LESLIE
MARTIN
MAURICE
NEIL
NORMAN
PETER
RANDOLPH
REGINALD
ROBIN
ROGER
ROLLIN
RONALD
ROY
SHAUN
STANLEY
STEPHEN
VICTOR

# THE ROYALS

Let's face it: Britain's royalty is our royalty too. After all, just compare the number of times American magazine covers have featured the sheepish smile of Queen Elizabeth's first daughter-in-law with those covers showing one of the Bush daughters-in-law. In a recent special "collector's edition," *People* magazine proclaimed this "The Decade of Diana." Not to mention Charles and Andrew and Fergie and Harry and Wills and Bea and Eugenie.

The transatlantic infatuation with British royal families dates back at least to the time of Queen Victoria and her nine children: Albert (later King Edward VII), Victoria (known as Princess Vicky), Alice, Alfred, Helena, Louise, Arthur, Leopold, and Beatrice. American fascination intensified during the 1930s and '40s when photos of The Little Princesses—sweet, serious Lilibet and the spunkier Margaret Rose—vied with Shirley Temple for space in *Life* and the *Saturday Evening Post*. The ensuing years brought Elizabeth's love match with Prince Philip and her coronation; Margaret's having to forsake her great love, the dashing but divorced fighter pilot Peter Townsend; and the deification of the Queen Mum. Then there were Elizabeth and Philip's "two families": Bonnie Prince Charlie and Princess Anne (once known as "Her Royal Haughtiness"), headline-making Randy Prince Andy (from Koo Stark to Sarah Ferguson—now rudely dubbed "Duchess of Do-Little" by the British tabloids), and theatrical brother Edward. And when Prince Charles married Lady Diana Spencer in 1981, it was the Americans who rose before dawn to drink in the pomp and circumstance.

Now, as the regal soap opera continues with the royal grandchildren, there is no doubt that the American audience will stay tuned.

# ROYAL FLUSH

**F**rom the Saxons to the Windsors, there have been about sixty-six monarchs of England, representing ten dynasties. The Saxons ruled from 802 (King Egbert) to 1066 (Harold II). Most of their names became the raw material for cartoons in *Punch* (especially the ones starting with Ethel—Ethelwulf, Ethelbald, Ethelbert, Ethelred), but a few have stood the test of time, namely:

| | |
|---|---|
| ALFRED | EDMUND |
| EDGAR | EDWARD |

Most of the female members of the Saxon dynasty fared no better in the name department than the men, with names also running toward hideous ones starting with the letter *E*: Elfweard, Edfleda, Ethelhilda, and Ethelfleda. The only two female royal names to survive from this period are:

| | |
|---|---|
| AGNES | EDITH |

The Norman Conquest added a Franco-Norse strain to the English bloodlines, and the following Normans and Plantagenets were found on the throne:

HENRY
JOHN
RICHARD
STEPHEN

WILLIAM (one of whom was called Rufus because of his red hair)

Their wives were named:

ADELA
BERENGARIA/
  BERENICE
ELEANOR
ISABEL

ISABELLA
MARGARET
MATILDA
PHILIPPA

Of these, the most popular among the extended royal family were Eleanor, Isabella, and Matilda. Other feminine names used during this period by the royals include:

ADELIZA
AGATHA
ALESIA
ALICE
AMICE
ARBELLA
AVELINE
BEATRICE
BLANCHE
BRIDGET
CECILY/CECILIA

CONSTANCE
EMMA
EUSTACIA
FRANCES
GERTRUDE
GRACE
IDA
JACQUETTA
JOAN
JUDITH
JULIANA

| | |
|---|---|
| LAURA | MURIEL |
| MARTHA | SIBYLLA |
| MARY | URSULA |

Norman and Plantagenet princes, earls, and dukes carried the following names:

| | |
|---|---|
| ANTHONY | HUMPHREY |
| ARCHIBALD | JASPER |
| ARTHUR | LIONEL |
| DAVID | MATTHEW |
| DUNCAN | NICHOLAS |
| EUSTACE | OTTO |
| GEOFFREY | PETER |
| GEORGE | REGINALD |
| GILBERT | ROBERT |
| GODWIN | ROGER |
| GUY | SIMON |
| HAMELIN | THEOBALD |
| HUGH | THOMAS |

Next came the Houses of Lancaster and York, which continued the hierarchy of Henrys, Edwards, and Richards. Their queens included:

| | |
|---|---|
| ANNE | JOAN |
| CATHERINE | MARY |
| ELIZABETH | |

The Tudors and Stuarts introduced four new royal male names:

| | |
|---|---|
| CHARLES | JAMES |
| GEORGE (husband of | PHILIP (husband of |
| Queen Anne) | Mary I) |

And the following females:

| | |
|---|---|
| ARABELLA | JANE |
| CHARLOTTE | LOUISA |
| HENRIETTA | SOPHIA |

The Hanovers, who included kings George I through IV, brought a Germanic influence to British royal names. Also, inevitably, the name Georgina entered the roster of royal females. Other feminine royal names used for the first time in this period include:

| | |
|---|---|
| AMELIA | OLIVIA |
| AUGUSTA | WILHELMINA |
| DOROTHEA | |

Besides George, in addition to the usual retinue of Charleses and Richards, three male names used for the first (and possibly the last) time in the royal family were:

| | |
|---|---|
| ADOLPHUS | OCTAVIUS |
| AUGUSTUS | |

Queen Victoria, granddaughter of George III and daughter of Edward, Duke of Kent, ascended to the throne in 1837 and reigned for sixty-three years. She was very concerned with the names of her descendants, particularly as an instrument of

**Charles the Promiscuous**

Charles II had sixteen illegitimate children, among them four named Charles and two named Charlotte.

preserving the memory of her beloved consort, Albert. In fact, if she had had her way, all her grandsons and great-grandsons would have been named Albert. Her own son Albert did name his first son Albert, but when he presumed to call his second George Frederick, she protested, "I fear I cannot admire the names you propose to give the Baby. I had hoped for some fine old name. Frederick is, however, the best of the two, and I hope you will call him so. George only came in with the Hanoverian family . . . Of course you will add Albert at the end, like your brothers, as you know we settled long ago that all dearest Papa's male descendants should bear that name, to mark our line, just as I wish all the girls to have Victoria after theirs."

She was still at it with the next generation. When her first great-grandson was born, Victoria wrote, "I am most anxious naturally that he should bear the name of his beloved Great Grandfather, a name which brought untold blessings to the whole Empire and that Albert should be his first name." This time, however, the parents prevailed, and the future Edward VIII was christened Edward Albert Christian George Andrew Patrick David.

**Fergie, However, Is Just Right**

*Private Eye,* the irreverent British magazine, sees the royal family as characters in a tawdry soap opera. Its less-than-royal nicknames for the players: The Queen and Prince Philip are called Brenda and Keith, Princess Margaret is Yvonne, and the Prince and Princess of Wales are known as Brian and Erica.

What follows is a list of names used by the royal family (in first, second, third, fourth, or fifth place) from Victoria to Princess Eugenie, including a few contemporary cousins. Like the dynasties of the past, the modern royals have continued some traditional royal names and introduced others. (To see what influence these names have on the population in general, see page 10.)

## F E M A L E

ADELAIDE
ALBERTA
ALEXANDRA
ALICE
AMELIA
ANNE
AUGUSTA
BEATRICE

BENEDIKTE
BIRGITTE
CAROLINE
CHARLOTTE
CLAUDINE
DAGMAR
DAVINA
ELLA

EUGENIE
FEODORE
GABRIELLA
HELEN
HELENA
JULIA
LOUISA
LOUISE
LUCY
MARGARET

MARINA
MARY
MAUD
MAY
OLGA
PAULINE
ROSE
SARAH
VICTORIA
ZARA

**M A L E**

ALBERT
ALFRED
ANDREW
ANTONY
ARTHUR
CHARLES
CHRISTIAN
DAVID
DUNCAN
EDMUND
EDWARD
ERNEST
FRANCIS
FRANKLIN
FREDERICK

GEORGE
HENRY/HARRY
JAMES
JOHN
LEOPOLD
LOUIS
MICHAEL
NICHOLAS
PATRICK
PAUL
PETER
PHILIP
RICHARD
VICTOR
WILLIAM

### The Alexandrine Age?

Perhaps Queen Victoria's obsession with the naming of her progeny can be traced back to the dispute over her own christening. According to Lytton Strachey in his biography of Victoria, her name became the focus of a power play between her father, the Duke of Kent, and his brother, the Prince Regent:

> . . . he (the Duke of Kent) would christen the child Elizabeth, a name of happy augury. In this, however, he reckoned without the Regent, who, seeing the chance of annoying his brother, suddenly announced that he himself would be present at the baptism, and signified . . . that one of the godfathers was to be the Emperor Alexander of Russia. And so when the ceremony took place, and the Archbishop of Canterbury asked by what name he was to baptise the child, the Regent replied "Alexandria." At this the Duke ventured to suggest that another name might be added. "Certainly," said the Regent; "Georgina?" "Or Elizabeth?" said the Duke. There was a pause, during which the Archbishop, with the baby in his lawn sleeves, looked with some uneasiness from one Prince to the other. "Very well, then," said the Regent at last, "call her after her mother. But Alexandrina must come first." Thus, to the disgust of her father, the child was christened Alexandrina Victoria.

Needless to say, the Russian name was dropped before long.

### But Elizabeth Krystle Kayla Debbie Doesn't Quite Make It

The more upper class you are, the more Christian names you have. Of the babies whose births were announced in *The London Times* in 1990, about 30 percent of the boys and 15 percent of the girls had three names each, while close to 10 percent of the children of both sexes were given four names—which gets you into royal territory. Who could forget Lady Diana tripping over Prince Charles's trail of names while making her wedding vows? Good thing she wasn't marrying Edward VIII, the king with the most names, at seven: Edward Albert Christian George Andrew Patrick David. Queen Mary, wife of George V, did him one better with eight names: Victoria Mary Augusta Louisa Olga Pauline Claudine Agnes. The next most name-heavy queen was Alexandra, consort of King Edward VII, with six names: Alexandra Caroline Mary Charlotte Louisa Julia. And King William IV's wife Adelaide had five: Adelaide Louisa Theresa Caroline Amelia.

One advantage to this plethora of middle names, apparently, is that you can honor an unroyal friend or relative or indulge a name fancy without mucking up the Royal Image. Witness the last four of Queen Mary's eight names, the pedestrian Olga, Pauline, Claudine, and Agnes. One of the Queen Mother's middle names is Angela, one of Prince Edward's is Antony, one of Lady Gabriella Windsor's is Ophelia, and one of Prince Michael of Kent's is Franklin, after his godfather, President Roosevelt.

# KING MACBETH AND OTHER SCOTTISH ROYALS

Until the first years of the seventeenth century, Scotland had its own royal family and its own set of royal names. There really was a King Macbeth in the Middle Ages, for instance. Some ancient royal Scottish names—Waltheof, for example, and Eochaid and Hextilda and Gruidh and Gruoch (Macbeth's queen)—are obsolete, and for good reason, today. But others survive and are well-used in Scotland and sometimes in the world at large.

Here, names of Scottish royals:

## FEMALE

AFRIKA
AMABEL
ANNABELLA
BETHOC

CHRISTINA/
  CHRISTIAN
DONADA
EUPHEMIA

FINNGHUALA/
   FINNUALA
HELEN
JANET
JEAN

MARGARET
MARJORIE (wildly pop-
   ular among four-
   teenth-century royals)
MATILDA

## M A L E

ALAN
ALEXANDER
ANDREW
ANGUS
ARCHIBALD
COLIN
CONSTANTINE
DAVID
DOLFIN
DONALD
DUFF
DUNCAN

DUNGAL
FINLAY
HAROLD
HUGH
KENNETH
MALCOLM
MALISE
NEIL
PATRICK
ROBERT
WALTER

# CLASS
# CONSCIOUSNESS

# SOCIAL STANDING

Ask an English parent about names, and he or she will start talking about class. More important than whether a name is in or out in Britain is whether it's considered upper class or not.

What determines a name's class standing? Consistent use by royalty automatically gives a name an upper-class seal of approval: Names such as Charles, Elizabeth, William, Henry, and Anne, conferred consistently on royal babies over the ages, are unimpeachably upper class. Other traditional royal names—Alexandra, Charlotte, Victoria, and James, for example—are well established on the upper-class roster. Even less traditional names borne by nobility—Diana, for instance, and Gabrielle and Marina and Angus and Zara—are now firmly upper class.

The most common royal names—Charles, Anne, William etc.—manage to be popular with all classes without losing an ounce of their upper-class weight. Less hefty royal names may not hold up as well to changes in locale and fashion: Angus, for instance, can be a working-class name in Scotland, and the popularity of Diana among the hoi polloi may eventually make that name common in both senses of the word.

---

### A Sloane by Any Other Name

Acceptable girls names include Emma, Lucinda, Sarah, Diana—and almost any name ending in "a" except Tanya, feminine derivatives of Henry, George or Charles: Henrietta, Harriet, Georgina, Charlotte, Caroline. Jolly-hockeysticks names: Jennifer, Jill, Judy (Gillian, Judith). Jane, plain or in combination (Sarah Jane, Eliza Jane). Mary and Anne are not very Sloane, more old dull aristocracy—Sloanes like some style and dash. Scottish names: Kirstie, Catriona, Fiona.

Boy Sloanes are called Henry, Charles, Mark, Peter, Simon, Christopher, Richard, William—what they call "plain English names" (actually Norman Conquistador names). Scottish Sloanes are called plain Scottish names: Andrew, Alistair, James, Alexander, Robert, Archie. Rupert came top in 1977, but Charles is the all-time favourite. Timothy and Jonathan are liked (John's a bit dull). . . .

In the garden of live flowers, Daisy, Flora and Pansy are Sloane; Lily and Heather are very unSloane. ("They christened her Marigold and hoped she would.")

—Ann Barr and Peter York, *The Official Sloane Ranger Handbook*

Other names are true class nomads: Harry and Abigail, for instance, once undeniably upper, became working class by the end of the nineteenth century, though now both have recovered favor with the upper classes. Samantha, an impeccably upper-class name thirty and forty years ago, became tarnished after it was popularized by the bewitched television character. Once a name becomes widely used by non-upper-class parents, upper-class ones stop using it until its widespread popularity has died down and it's once again "safe" to name the little honorable Patrick or Rose or Harry without

---

**Must Be the Sun**

The infant (who was killed) has a most peculiar name, Azaria: something really fishy about that zed. We were fascinated.

I asked Chamberlain about her predilection for quirky names: she replied that such outlandish ones are commonplace in Australia. "Kylie," she said, "is a really old-fashioned, traditional name in Australia." Azaria's full name had been Azaria Chantel Loren, and the Chamberlains thought up some equally fanciful names for their second daughter: Kahlia Shonell Nikari. "The meaning of Shonell I have never been able to discover," she writes in her book, "but it's French I think."

—Valerie Grove on Lindy Chamberlain (mother of the "dingo baby," who was portrayed by Meryl Streep in the film *Cry in the Dark*), *The London Times,* January 27, 1991

fearing someone will mistake him for a charwoman's child.

The workings of class nomadism may account for the fact that some of the most thoroughly upper-class names are those so stodgy—and, some may say, ugly—that they will never be in danger of becoming common. More than one British parent, for instance, has said that the most upper class name you can give your daughter is Henrietta. Eugenie qualifies for the same reasons. And for boys, Hugh and Piers are right up there along with Hamish.

A name can be counted as upper or not depending on niceties (or not) of spelling. Deborah, Geoffrey, and Stephen, for instance, are upper class; Debra, Jeffrey, and Steven decidedly non. In fact, any variant spelling—Martyn instead of Martin, Judyth instead of Judith—can signal a perfectly respectable name's fall from grace. Likewise, nicknames can make the difference in a name's class status: Kitty is an upper-class nickname for Katherine while Kath is non-upper; Ned is an accepted upper-class abbreviation for Edward, Ed and Eddie are non. And pronunciation can be significant: Ralph, pronounced "Rafe," is U; pronounced "Ralf," as in "Kramden," is non-U, to use the terms coined by Nancy Mitford in her influential mid-fifties essay.

As a general rule, "old" names are upper class and "new" names are not. Many U names—especially girls' names such as Clarissa, Minerva, Pamela, and Vanessa—were already popular in the seventeenth and eighteenth centuries, a period that was good to the upper classes in England. On the other hand, names popularized in recent years by movie or rock stars or soap opera characters—what the English sniffingly and often erroneously call "American" names—are non-upper. The girls' names Sharon and Tracy, for reasons largely mysterious to the American observer, are thought of as working-class caricatures, the lowest of the low. So too is the new hit name Kylie, after Australian singer and Barbie lookalike Kylie Minogue. For boys, names that amount to working-class markers include Wayne, Craig, and, yes, Jason.

Rather than divide the following names into three categories—for upper, middle, and lower classes—we've relied on Mitford's infamous designations. In a treatise that still causes ripples in English society, Mitford defined various terms as either U (upper class) or non-U. In general, according to Mitford, the non-upper classes favor the fancy while the upper classes call a spade a spade. The non-U term is "home," says Mitford, while the U one is "house"; non-U's say "serviette," U's say "napkin." And, it follows, a non-U name is Heather, and a U one is Henrietta.

## G I R L S

### U

ABIGAIL
ALEXANDRA
ALICE
ALLEGRA
AMANDA
AMELIA
ANASTASIA
ANNA
ANNABEL
ANNE
ANTHEA
ANTONIA
ARABELLA
ARAMINTA
AUGUSTA
BEATRICE
BELINDA
BRENDA
CAMILLA
CAROLINE
CATHERINE
CECILY

| | |
|---|---|
| CHARLOTTE | GRACE |
| CHLOE | HANNAH |
| CLARE | HARRIET |
| CLARISSA | HELEN |
| CLEMENTINE | HENRIETTA |
| CONSTANCE | HILARY |
| CORDELIA | HONOR |
| CORNELIA | HOPE |
| CRESSIDA | IMOGEN |
| DAPHNE | INDIA |
| DEBORAH | IONA |
| DELILAH | ISABEL(LE) |
| DIANA | ISADORA |
| DINAH | JANE |
| EDITH | JEMIMA |
| EDWINA | JESSAMINE |
| ELEANOR | JESSAMY |
| ELIZA | JESSICA |
| ELIZABETH | JOAN |
| EMILY | JOANNA |
| EMMA | JOSEPHINE |
| EUGENIE | JUDITH |
| FAITH | JULIA |
| FELICITY | JULIET |
| FIONA | KATE |
| FLORA | KATHERINE |
| FRANCES | KAY |
| FRANCESCA | KEZIAH |
| FREDERICA | LARISSA |
| GABRIELLE | LAURA |
| GEMMA | LEONORA |
| GEORGIA | LOUISE |
| GEORGINA | LUCINDA |

| | |
|---|---|
| LUCY | PRIMROSE |
| MADELEINE | PRISCILLA |
| MARGARET | PRUDENCE |
| MARIA | REBECCA |
| MARIGOLD | ROSE |
| MARIS(S)A | ROSEMARY |
| MARTHA | RUTH |
| MARY | SABRINA |
| MEG | SARAH |
| MELISSA | SELENA |
| MINERVA | SERAPHINA |
| MIRANDA | SOPHIA |
| NATALIE | SOPHIE |
| NATASHA | STEPHANIE |
| NICOLA | SUSANNA(H) |
| NORA | TABITHA |
| OLIVIA | TAMARA |
| PAMELA | TAMSIN |
| PANDORA | THEODORA |
| PANSY | VANESSA |
| PENELOPE | VICTORIA |
| PHILIPPA | VIOLET |
| PIPPA | VIRGINIA |
| POLLY | WINIFRED |
| POPPY | ZARA |

## N O N - U

| | |
|---|---|
| ALEXIS | ANNETTE |
| ALLY | APRIL |
| ANGELA | ASHLEY |

| | |
|---|---|
| AUDREY | JANINE |
| BARBIE | JILLY |
| BEVERLY | JOYCE |
| BRANDI | KATHLEEN |
| CAITLIN | KATHRYN |
| CANDACE | KELLY |
| CARLA | KERRY |
| CARLY | KIMBERLY |
| CHARLENE | KYLIE |
| CHELSEA | LOIS |
| CHERYL | LORETTA |
| COLLEEN | LORRAINE |
| CRYSTAL | LYNN |
| DANIELLE | MADGE |
| DARLENE | MANDY |
| DAWN | MARCIA |
| DEANNE/A | MARILYN |
| DEBRA | MEGAN |
| DENA | MELANIE |
| DENISE | MICHELLE |
| DIANE | MINDY |
| DOLLY | NICOLE |
| DONNA | NOREEN |
| DOREEN | NORMA |
| DORIS | PATTY |
| EILEEN | PAULINE |
| ERIN | PHYLLIS |
| FALLON | RHODA |
| FAWN | RHONDA |
| GLORIA | RICKI |
| HAYLEY | ROCHELLE |
| HEATHER | RUBY |
| IRENE | SHANNON |

| | |
|---|---|
| SHARON | TINA |
| SHEILA | TRACY |
| SHELLEY | TRISH |
| SHERRY | VALERIE |
| SHIRLEY | YVETTE |
| STACY | YVONNE |

## B O Y S

### U

| | |
|---|---|
| ADRIAN | COLIN |
| ALARIC | CRISPIN |
| ALEXANDER | CYRIL |
| ALISTAIR | DAVID |
| AMBROSE | DOMINIC(K) |
| ANDREW | DUNCAN |
| ANGUS | EDWARD |
| ANTHONY | EUGENE |
| ARCHIE | FELIX |
| AUBREY | FRANCIS |
| BASIL | FREDERICK |
| BENEDICT | GARETH |
| BEVIS | GEOFFREY |
| CASPER | GILES |
| CECIL | GRAHAM |
| CEDRIC | GREGORY |
| CHARLES | HAMISH |
| CHRISTIAN | HARRY |
| CHRISTOPHER | HENRY |

HUGH
HUGO
IAN
JAGO
JAMES
JAMIE
JOHN
JULIAN
LACHLAM
LAWRENCE
LEO
LESLIE
LOUIS
MALCOLM
MARTIN
NED
NICHOLAS
NIGEL
NOEL
OLIVER
ORLANDO

PATRICK
PAUL
PEREGRINE
PIERS
QUENTIN/QUINTON
RALPH
REGGIE
ROBIN
RORY
RUPERT
ST. JOHN
SEBASTIAN
SIMON
STEPHEN
TARQUIN
THEODORE
THOMAS
TIMOTHY
TORQUIL
TREVOR
WILLIAM

## N O N - U

ARNOLD
BERT
BRANDON
BRETT
BRICE
BRUCE
CARL

CHAD
CLIFFORD
CRAIG
DARREN
DARRYL
DENNIS
DES

| | |
|---|---|
| DESMOND | LEE |
| DIRK | MAURICE |
| DONALD | NORMAN |
| DOUG | RICK |
| DWAYNE | RODNEY |
| ED/EDDIE | RONALD |
| GARY | SCOTT |
| GLENN | SHANE |
| JASON | STANLEY |
| JEFFREY | STEVEN |
| JODY | TODD |
| JON | TRACY |
| KEITH | VERNON |
| KENNETH | VICTOR |
| KEVIN | VINCENT |
| KYLE | WARREN |
| LANCE | WAYNE |
| LARRY | |

# THE BARMAIDS

When British comedienne Tracey Ullman named her little girl Mable, and rock 'n' roller Bob Geldof called his three daughters Fifi Trixiebelle, Peaches, and Little Pixie, we smelled a trend. It was the return of the name of the cheeky old British barmaid, who's ready to call out your order for a pint of bitter in her best East London accent:

| | |
|---|---|
| ANGIE | GERT |
| ANNIE | GINGER |
| AUDREY | GRACIE |
| DAISY | JILLY |
| DOLLY | KITTY |
| DOT | LILY |
| DULCIE | LOLA |
| ELSIE | MABEL |
| FLO | MADGE |
| FLORRIE | MAISIE |
| FLOSSIE | MANDY |

| MARGE | RITA |
|-------|------|
| MAUDIE | ROSIE |
| MILLY | RUBY |
| MOLLY | SADIE |
| NELL | SAL |
| PATSY | TESS |
| PEG | TRIXIE |
| POLLY | VI |
| PRU | VIV |
| QUEENIE | WINNIE |

Among the surprising ups and downs in the histories of names Jane has had her share. At one period she was accustomed to sleep in a grand bedroom and dine at very high tables, but in the nineteenth century she was likely to climb up countless stairs to her menials' attic at night and to go to the basement for her meals.

—Ivor Brown, *A Charm of Names*

"I grew up with Jilly and Tamsin driving Volvos," says (Tracey) Ullman, slipping into the Queen's English. "But I wasn't one of them. . . . I always felt more comfortable with Cockney and working-class people."

—Interview in *Los Angeles Times,* March 3, 1991

"What a grand name it is—Gaisford Arthur Brandreth Forbes," said Dulcie. "Surely he *must* have been of noble birth?"

—Barbara Pym, *No Fond Return of Love*

CECILY: . . . It had always been a girlish dream of mine to love some one whose name was Ernest. . . . There is something in that name that seems to inspire absolute confidence. I pity any poor married woman whose husband is not called Ernest.

ALGERNON: . . . do you mean to say you could not love me if I had some other name?

CECILY: But what name?

ALGERNON: Oh, any name you like—Algernon—for instance.

CECILY: But I don't like the name of Algernon.

ALGERNON: . . . I really can't see why you should object to the name of Algernon. It is not a bad name. In fact, it is rather an aristocratic name. Half of the chaps who get into the Bankruptcy Court are called Algernon.

—Oscar Wilde, *The Importance of Being Earnest*

# LITERARY
# LIGHTS

An anglophile, almost by definition, is a lover not only of British people but also of British literature. And nearly every one we've ever known has one particular passion, be it Shakespeare, the Metaphysical poets—Donne, Marvell, Herrick, *et al.*—Jane Austen, Dickens, George Eliot, Thomas Hardy, Evelyn Waugh, or Martin Amis.

And one significant element, we think, is the names of their characters, names you just wouldn't find anywhere else. Ebenezer Scrooge. Eustacia Vye. Miles Malpractice.

We have zeroed in on a few of these provinces that we consider especially rich fields to mine, with a miscellany at the end to take in everyone from Sir Walter Scott to Stevie Smith.

# KNAMES OF THE ROUND TABLE

And what could be more noble than a name that has known Camelot? Herewith some names from the Arthurian legend:

## FEMALE

ELAINE          ISOLDE
ENID            MORGAN
GUINEVERE

## MALE

ARTHUR          GALAHAD
BEDIVERE        GARETH
BORS            GAWAIN

KAY  
LAUNCELOT/  
   LANCELOT  
MARK

MERLIN  
PELLEAS  
PERCIVAL  
TRISTRAM

# SHAKESPEARE, THE BARD OF NAMING

William Shakespeare drew upon many sources of inspiration, both historical and fictional, for his characters, including Holinshead's *Chronicles*, Plutarch's *Lives*, and Boccaccio's *Decameron*. But the Bard, surprisingly enough, has not had as much influence on naming as might have been expected. Perhaps we can rectify this by considering:

## F E M A L E

| | |
|---|---|
| ADRIANA | *The Comedy of Errors* |
| BEATRICE | *Much Ado About Nothing* |
| BIANCA | *The Taming of the Shrew; Othello* |
| CASSANDRA | *Troilus and Cressida* |
| CELIA | *As You Like It* |
| CHARMIAN | *Antony and Cleopatra* |
| CORDELIA | *King Lear* |
| CRESSIDA | *Troilus and Cressida* |

| | |
|---|---|
| DESDEMONA | *Othello* |
| DIANA | *All's Well That Ends Well* |
| DORCAS | *The Winter's Tale* |
| EMILIA | *Othello; The Winter's Tale* |
| HELENA | *A Midsummer Night's Dream; All's Well That Ends Well* |
| IMOGEN | *Cymbeline* |
| ISABEL | *Henry V* |
| ISABELLA | *Measure for Measure* |
| JACQUENETTA | *Love's Labour's Lost* |
| JESSICA | *The Merchant of Venice* |
| JULIA | *Two Gentlemen of Verona* |
| JULIET | *Romeo and Juliet* |
| JUNO | *The Tempest* |
| LAVINIA | *Titus Andronicus* |
| LUCIANA | *The Comedy of Errors* |
| MARINA | *Pericles* |
| MIRANDA | *The Tempest* |
| NERISSA | *The Merchant of Venice* |
| OCTAVIA | *Antony and Cleopatra* |
| OLIVIA | *Twelfth Night* |
| OPHELIA | *Hamlet* |
| PAULINA | *The Winter's Tale* |
| PERDITA | *The Winter's Tale* |
| PHEBE | *As You Like It* |
| PORTIA | *The Merchant of Venice; Julius Caesar* |
| REGAN | *King Lear* |
| ROSALIND | *As You Like It* |
| ROSALINE | *Love's Labour's Lost* |
| TAMORA | *Titus Andronicus* |
| TITANIA | *A Midsummer Night's Dream* |
| VIOLA | *Twelfth Night* |

## M  A  L  E

| | |
|---|---|
| ADRIAN . . . . . . . . . . . | *The Tempest* |
| ALONSO . . . . . . . . . . | *The Tempest* |
| ANGUS . . . . . . . . . . . | *Macbeth* |
| ANTONIO . . . . . . . . . | *The Tempest; Two Gentlemen of Verona; The Merchant of Venice; Much Ado About Nothing* |
| BALTHASAR . . . . . . . | *Romeo and Juliet; The Merchant of Venice; Much Ado About Nothing* |
| BALTHAZAR . . . . . . . | *A Comedy of Errors* |
| BENEDICK . . . . . . . . . | *Much Ado About Nothing* |
| CLAUDIO . . . . . . . . . | *Measure for Measure; Much Ado About Nothing* |
| CLEON . . . . . . . . . . . . | *Pericles* |
| CORIN . . . . . . . . . . . . | *As You Like It* |
| CORNELIUS . . . . . . . . | *Hamlet* |
| DION . . . . . . . . . . . . . | *The Winter's Tale* |
| DUNCAN . . . . . . . . . | *Macbeth* |
| FABIAN . . . . . . . . . . . | *Twelfth Night* |
| FRANCISCO . . . . . . . . | *Hamlet* |
| GREGORY . . . . . . . . . | *Romeo and Juliet* |
| HORATIO . . . . . . . . . | *Hamlet* |
| HUMPHREY . . . . . . . . | *Henry VI, Part II* |
| LORENZO . . . . . . . . . | *The Merchant of Venice* |
| LUCIUS . . . . . . . . . . . | *Timon of Athens; Titus Andronicus; Julius Caesar* |
| MALCOLM . . . . . . . . . | *Macbeth* |
| OLIVER . . . . . . . . . . . | *As You Like It* |
| ORLANDO . . . . . . . . . | *As You Like It* |
| OWEN . . . . . . . . . . . . | *Henry IV, Part I* |
| PHILO . . . . . . . . . . . . | *Antony and Cleopatra* |
| SAMPSON . . . . . . . . . | *Romeo and Juliet* |
| SEBASTIAN . . . . . . . . | *Twelfth Night; The Tempest* |
| TIMON . . . . . . . . . . . | *Measure for Measure* |
| TOBY . . . . . . . . . . . . | *Twelfth Night* |

In the imaginative comedies of his later years the poet could be an innovator for the heroines. Miranda, she who must be admired, seems to have been his own invention for *The Tempest*. . . . Perdita, the lost one, is fitted to the events of *A Winter's Tale*. Marina in *Pericles* is also a 'plot name', since she was born at sea.

—Ivor Brown, *A Charm of Names*

# THE METAPHYSICAL/ PASTORAL POETS

**P**oets have always harkened back to earlier times to invoke the classical muse, and this was certainly true of the seventeenth-century English poets. Here are a few of the evocative names they used for their coy mistresses:

ALTHEA . . . . . . . . . . Richard Lovelace
AMARANTHA . . . . . . Richard Lovelace
ANTHEA . . . . . . . . . . Robert Herrick
CELIA . . . . . . . . . . . . . Ben Jonson, Thomas Carew
CHLORIS . . . . . . . . . . . Edmund Waller
CORINNA . . . . . . . . . Robert Herrick
CYNTHIA . . . . . . . . . . Ben Jonson
ELECTRA . . . . . . . . . . Robert Herrick
ELISA . . . . . . . . . . . . . Abraham Cowley
GRATIANA . . . . . . . . . Richard Lovelace
HELEONORA . . . . . . . Alexander Cowley
ISABELLA . . . . . . . . . . Abraham Cowley

JULIA .............. Robert Herrick
JULIANA ........... Andrew Marvell
LUCASTA .......... Richard Lovelace
MARGARITA ....... Abraham Cowley
MYRHA ............ Robert Herrick
PERILLA ............ Robert Herrick
SAPHO ............. Robert Herrick
THOMASINE ....... Abraham Cowley

# JANE AUSTEN

The self-contained county canvases of Jane Austen are populated with marriagable daughters, meddling mothers, and suitable suitors, all bearing such sensible and not-so-sensible names as:

## F E M A L E

| | |
|---|---|
| ALICIA . . . . . . . . . . . . | *Persuasion* |
| ANNAMARIA . . . . . . . | *Sense and Sensibility* |
| ANNE . . . . . . . . . . . . . | *Persuasion* |
| AUGUSTA . . . . . . . . . | *Emma* |
| CAROLINE . . . . . . . . . | *Pride and Prejudice* |
| CATHARINE (KITTY) | *Pride and Prejudice* |
| CATHERINE . . . . . . . . | *Northanger Abbey* |
| CHARLOTTE . . . . . . . | *Pride and Prejudice; Northanger Abbey; Sanditon; Sense and Sensibility* |
| CLARA . . . . . . . . . . . . | *Sanditon* |

DIANA ............. Sanditon
ELEANOR .......... Northanger Abbey
ELINOR ............ Sense and Sensibility
ELIZA ............. Sense and Sensibility
ELIZABETH ........ Pride and Prejudice; Persuasion
EMMA ............. Emma
ESTHER ............ Sanditon
FANNY ............. Sense and Sensibility; Mansfield Park
GEORGIANA ....... Pride and Prejudice
HARRIET ........... Emma
ISABELLA .......... Emma; Northanger Abbey
JANE .............. Pride and Prejudice; Emma
JEMIMA ............ Persuasion
JULIA ............. Mansfield Park
LETITIA ........... Sanditon
LOUISA ............ Persuasion
LUCY .............. Mansfield Park; Sense and Sensibility
LYDIA ............. Pride and Prejudice
MARGARET ........ Sense and Sensibility
MARIA ............. Mansfield Park
MARIANNE ......... Sense and Sensibility
MARY .............. Persuasion
PENELOPE .......... Persuasion
SARAH (SALLY) ..... Northanger Abbey
SELINA ............. Emma
SUSAN ............. Sanditon; Mansfield Park

## M A L E

CHARLES .......... Pride and Prejudice; Persuasion
DARCY (surname) .... Pride and Prejudice
EDMUND ........... Mansfield Park
EDWARD .......... Sense and Sensibility
FITZWILLIAM ....... Pride and Prejudice

FRANK ............. *Emma*
FREDERICK ......... *Persuasion*
HARRY ............. *Persuasion*
HENRY ............. *Mansfield Park; Northanger Abbey*
HUGH ............. *Northanger Abbey*
JAMES ............. *Northanger Abbey*
PHILIP ............. *Emma*
SIDNEY ............ *Sanditon*
WALTER ........... *Persuasion*
WILLIAM ........... *Persuasion*

# NINETEENTH-CENTURY REVIVAL

**M**any of the names we think of as long used in England in fact fell out of favor—sometimes to the point of obsolescence—for several centuries, only to be reintroduced by the religious and literary movements of the nineteenth century, according to Withycombe's *Oxford Dictionary of English Christian Names*.

The Romantic movement and the works of Sir Walter Scott had revived the name Amy for girls, as well as the following for boys:

| | |
|---|---|
| GUY | ROLAND |
| NIGEL | WILFRID |
| QUENTIN | |

The Tractarian movement reintroduced some long-bypassed saints' names for boys:

| | |
|---|---|
| AIDAN | BENEDICT |
| ALBAN | BERNARD |
| AUGUSTINE | THEODORE |

Tennyson and the pre-Raphaelite medievalists breathed new life into the following names:

### G I R L S

| | |
|---|---|
| ALICE | ELLA |
| EDITH | |

### B O Y S

| | |
|---|---|
| HUGH | ROGER |
| LANCELOT | WALTER |
| RALPH | |

# DICKENSIANS

Probably the supreme name-master of English or any other culture was Charles John Huffam Dickens. And while he did in the main draw from the common stock of names, he also had a fine ear for the unusual (e.g., Quebec), as well as a genius for the combination of first and family names. In fact this is one of the rare cases in our books in which we wish we included surnames.

## FEMALE

| | |
|---|---|
| ABBEY | *Our Mutual Friend* |
| ADA | *Bleak House* |
| ALICE | *Dombey and Son* |
| AMY | *Little Dorrit* |
| ANASTASIA | *Our Mutual Friend* |
| ARABELLA | *The Pickwick Papers* |
| BELLA | *Our Mutual Friend* |

| | |
|---|---|
| BETSEY | *David Copperfield* |
| CECILIA | *Hard Times; Our Mutual Friend* |
| CHARITY (CHERRY). | *Martin Chuzzlewit* |
| CHARLOTTE (CHARLEY) | *Bleak House* |
| CLARA | *David Copperfield, Great Expectations* |
| CLARISSA | *David Copperfield* |
| DOLLY | *Barnaby Rudge* |
| DORA | *David Copperfield* |
| EDITH | *Dombey and Son* |
| EMILY | *David Copperfield* |
| ESTELLA | *Great Expectations* |
| ESTHER | *Bleak House* |
| FANNY | *Dombey and Son; Little Dorrit* |
| FLORA | *Little Dorrit* |
| FLORENCE | *Dombey and Son* |
| GEORGIANA | *Our Mutual Friend* |
| HARRIET | *Little Dorrit* |
| HELENA | *The Mystery of Edwin Drood* |
| HENRIETTA | *Our Mutual Friend; Nicholas Nickleby* |
| HONORIA | *Bleak House* |
| JENNY | *Our Mutual Friend* |
| JOSEPHINE | *Hard Times* |
| JULIA | *David Copperfield* |
| KATE | *Nicholas Nickleby* |
| LAVINIA | *David Copperfield; Our Mutual Friend* |
| LIZZIE | *Our Mutual Friend* |
| LOUISA | *Dombey and Son; Hard Times* |
| LUCIE | *A Tale of Two Cities* |
| LUCRETIA | *Dombey and Son* |
| MADELINE | *Nicholas Nickleby* |
| MALTA | *Bleak House* |
| MARGARETTA | *Our Mutual Friend* |
| MARTHA | *The Pickwick Papers; Barnaby Rudge; David Copperfield* |
| MATILDA | *Nicholas Nickleby* |

Dickens chose to name his own children after famous literary lights. His seven sons were Alfred Tennyson Dickens, Francis Jeffrey Dickens, Henry Fielding Dickens, Sydney Smith Haldimand Dickens, Walter Landor Dickens, Edward Bulwer Lytton Dickens, and—immodestly including himself—Charles Culliford Boz Dickens. Not surprisingly, he almost immediately gave each a nickname.

| | |
|---|---|
| MERCY (MERRY) .... | *Martin Chuzzlewit* |
| MINNIE ............ | *Little Dorrit* |
| NANCY ............ | *Oliver Twist* |
| NELL .............. | *The Old Curiosity Shop* |
| PLEASANT ........ | *Our Mutual Friend* |
| RACHAEL .......... | *Hard Times* |
| ROSA ............. | *David Copperfield; Bleak House; The Mystery of Edwin Drood* |
| ROSE ............. | *Oliver Twist* |
| SARAH ............ | *Martin Chuzzlewit* |
| SOPHIA ........... | *The Old Curiosity Shop* |
| SOPHRONIA ....... | *Our Mutual Friend; The Old Curiosity Shop* |
| SUSAN ............ | *Dombey and Son* |
| VOLUMNIA ........ | *Bleak House* |

## M A L E

ALEXANDER ....... *A Tale of Two Cities*
ALLAN ............. *Bleak House*
ANTHONY ......... *The Pickwick Papers; Martin Chuzzlewit*
AUGUSTUS ........ *The Pickwick Papers; Martin Chuzzlewit*
BARNABY .......... *Barnaby Rudge*
BARNEY ............ *Oliver Twist*
BARTHOLOMEW .... *Bleak House*
BAYHAM .......... *Bleak House*
BENJAMIN .......... *Martin Chuzzlewit*
BRADLEY .......... *Our Mutual Friend*
CHEVY ............. *Martin Chuzzlewit*
CHRISTOPHER (KIT). *The Old Curiosity Shop; Little Dorrit*
DANIEL ............ *The Old Curiosity Shop; Little Dorrit*
DAVID ............. *David Copperfield*
EBENEZER .......... *A Christmas Carol*
EDWIN ............. *The Mystery of Edwin Drood*
ELIJAH ............. *Martin Chuzzlewit*
EPHRAIM ........... *Little Dorrit*
EUGENE .......... *Our Mutual Friend*
FERDINAND ........ *Little Dorrit*
FREDERICK ......... *Little Dorrit*
GABRIEL ........... *The Pickwick Papers; Barnaby Rudge*
GEOFFREY ......... *Barnaby Rudge*
HIRAM ............. *The Mystery of Edwin Drood*
HORATIO .......... *The Pickwick Papers*
ISAAC ............. *The Old Curiosity Shop*
JACOB ............. *A Christmas Carol*
JARVIS ............. *A Tale of Two Cities*
JEM ............... *The Pickwick Papers*
JEREMIAH .......... *Little Dorrit*
JESSE ............. *Our Mutual Friend*
JONAS ............. *Martin Chuzzlewit*
JOSHUA ............ *Bleak House*

| | |
|---|---|
| JOSIAH . . . . . . . . . . . . | *Hard Times* |
| LAWRENCE . . . . . . . . | *Bleak House* |
| MARK . . . . . . . . . . . . . | *Barnaby Rudge* |
| MARTIN . . . . . . . . . . | *Martin Chuzzlewit* |
| MATHEW . . . . . . . . . . | *Great Expectations* |
| MATTHEW . . . . . . . . . | *Nicholas Nickleby; Bleak House* |
| NATHANIEL . . . . . . . . | *The Pickwick Papers* |
| NICHOLAS . . . . . . . . . | *Nicholas Nickleby* |
| NICODEMUS . . . . . . . | *Our Mutual Friend* |
| NOAH . . . . . . . . . . . . | *Oliver Twist* |
| OLIVER . . . . . . . . . . . | *Oliver Twist* |
| PARKER . . . . . . . . . . . | *Dombey and Son* |
| PAUL . . . . . . . . . . . . . | *Martin Chuzzlewit; Dombey and Son* |
| PETER . . . . . . . . . . . . | *The Pickwick Papers* |
| PHILIP (PIP) . . . . . . . . | *Great Expectations* |
| QUEBEC . . . . . . . . . . | *Bleak House* |
| RALPH . . . . . . . . . . . . | *Nicholas Nickleby* |
| REGINALD . . . . . . . . | *Our Mutual Friend* |
| ROGER . . . . . . . . . . . . | *A Tale of Two Cities* |
| SAMPSON . . . . . . . . . | *The Old Curiosity Shop* |
| SAMUEL . . . . . . . . . . | *The Pickwick Papers* |
| SEPTIMUS . . . . . . . . . | *The Mystery of Edwin Drood* |
| SETH . . . . . . . . . . . . . | *Martin Chuzzlewit* |
| SILAS . . . . . . . . . . . . . | *Our Mutual Friend* |
| SIMON (SIM) . . . . . . . . | *Barnaby Rudge* |
| SOLOMON . . . . . . . . . | *The Pickwick Papers; Dombey and Son; A Tale of Two Cities* |
| STEPHEN . . . . . . . . . . | *Hard Times* |
| SYDNEY . . . . . . . . . . . | *A Tale of Two Cities* |
| TIM . . . . . . . . . . . . . . | *Nicholas Nickleby, A Christmas Carol* |
| TOBY . . . . . . . . . . . . . | *Oliver Twist* |
| TRACY . . . . . . . . . . . . | *The Pickwick Papers* |
| URIAH . . . . . . . . . . . . | *David Copperfield* |
| VINCENT . . . . . . . . . . | *Nicholas Nickleby* |
| WALTER . . . . . . . . . . | *Nicholas Nickleby; Dombey and Son* |
| WATT . . . . . . . . . . . . . | *Bleak House* |
| ZEPHANIAH . . . . . . . . | *Martin Chuzzlewit* |

He was shy, and unwilling to own to the name of Reginald, as being too aspiring and self-assertive a name. In his signature he used only the initial R., and imparted what it really stood for, to none but chosen friends, under the seal of confidence.

—Charles Dickens, *Our Mutual Friend*

# WAUGH, WODEHOUSE, AND PYM

---

Of all the modern English writers, none has been so English as Evelyn Waugh, P. G. Wodehouse, and Barbara Pym, each of whom has been a master at naming characters. Here we offer a selective (after all, Wodehouse did write more than one hundred novels and stories) sampling:

## F E M A L E

| | | |
|---|---|---|
| AGATHA | Waugh | *Vile Bodies* |
| ALLEGRA | Pym | *Excellent Women* |
| ANTHEA | Pym | *Cramton Hodnet* |
| AVICE | Pym | *A Few Green Leaves* |
| BEATRIX | Pym | *A Few Green Leaves* |
| BERYL | Waugh | *Brideshead Revisited* |
| CHASTITY | Waugh | *Vile Bodies* |
| CHRISTABEL | Pym | *A Few Green Leaves* |

| CLARICE | Wodehouse | Lord Emsworth and Others; Mulliner Nights |
|---|---|---|
| CORDELIA | Waugh | Brideshead Revisited |
| CRESSIDA | Pym | An Academic Question |
| DAHLIA | Wodehouse | Lord Emsworth and Others |
| DAPHNE | Pym | A Few Green Leaves |
| DOMENICA | Waugh | Unconditional Surrender |
| DULCIE | Pym | No Fond Return of Love |
| EVANGELINE | Wodehouse | Lord Emsworth and Others; Mulliner Nights |
| FAITH | Waugh | Vile Bodies |
| FLAVIA | Pym | A Few Green Leaves |
| FORTITUDE | Waugh | Vile Bodies |
| GRAYCE | Wodehouse | The Luck of the Bodkins |
| HELENA | Pym | Excellent Women |
| HERMIONE | Pym | No Fond Return of Love |
| HYPATIA | Wodehouse | Mulliner Nights |
| JUSTICE | Waugh | Vile Bodies |
| KERSTIE | Waugh | Unconditional Surrender |
| MAGDALEN | Pym | A Few Green Leaves |
| MARCELLA | Wodehouse | Mulliner Nights |
| MARIGOLD | Pym | Quartet in Autumn |
| MENNA | Pym | An Academic Question |
| MERCY | Waugh | Vile Bodies |
| PERDITA | Waugh | Unconditional Surrender |
| PHILIPPA | Waugh | Brideshead Revisited |
| PRIMROSE | Pym | Less Than Angels |
| PRISCILLA | Pym | Quartet in Autumn |
| PRUDENCE | Waugh | Vile Bodies |
|  | Pym | Jane and Prudence |
| TAMSIN | Pym | A Few Green Leaves |
| THEODORA | Waugh | The Loved One |
| URSULA | Waugh | Vile Bodies |
| VIOLET/VIOLA | Pym | No Fond Return of Love |
| WINIFRED | Pym | Excellent Women |
| ZITA | Waugh | Officers and Gentlemen |

# M A L E

| | | |
|---|---|---|
| ALARIC | Pym | *Less Than Angels* |
| AMBROSE | Wodehouse | *The Luck of the Bodkins* |
| | Waugh | *The Loved One* |
| ANGUS | Waugh | *Officers and Gentlemen* |
| ARCHIBALD | Wodehouse | *Indiscretions of Archie* |
| AUGUSTINE | Wodehouse | *Mulliner Nights* |
| AYLWIN | Pym | *No Fond Return of Love* |
| BASIL | Waugh | *Black Mischief* |
| CRISPIN | Pym | *An Academic Question* |
| CYRIL | Wodehouse | *Mulliner Nights* |
| DIGBY | Pym | *Less Than Angels* |
| DUNCAN | Waugh | *Officers and Gentlemen* |
| EGBERT | Wodehouse | *Mulliner Nights* |
| EPHRAIM | Pym | *Less Than Angels* |
| EUSTACE | Wodehouse | *Mulliner Nights* |
| EVERAND | Waugh | *Unconditional Surrender* |
| EVERARD | Pym | *Excellent Women* |
| FELIX | Waugh | *Officers and Gentlemen* |
| | Pym | *Less Than Angels* |
| GERVASE | Waugh | *Unconditional Surrender* |
| GILES | Pym | *Less Than Angels* |
| GUY | Waugh | *Unconditional Surrender;* |
| | | *Officers and Gentlemen* |
| HUMPHREY | Waugh | *Decline and Fall* |
| IVOR | Wodehouse | *The Luck of the Bodkins* |
| | Waugh | *Officers and Gentlemen* |
| JASPER | Wodehouse | *Mulliner Nights* |
| JOCELYN | Waugh | *A Handful of Dust* |
| LANCELOT | Wodehouse | *Mulliner Nights* |
| MELCHIOR | Waugh | *Brideshead Revisited* |
| MONTAGUE | Wodehouse | *The Luck of the Bodkins* |
| NEVILLE | Pym | *No Fond Return of Love* |
| NIGEL | Pym | *Quartet in Autumn* |
| ORLANDO | Wodehouse | *Mulliner Nights* |

| | | |
|---|---|---|
| OTTO | Waugh | *Decline and Fall* |
| PERCY | Wodehouse | *Mulliner Nights* |
| | Waugh | *Black Mischief* |
| PEREGRINE | Waugh | *Unconditional Surrender* |
| REGINALD | Wodehouse | *Mulliner Nights* |
| REX | Waugh | *Black Mischief* |
| | Waugh | *Brideshead Revisited* |
| ROCKINGHAM | Pym | *Excellent Women* |
| RODNEY | Wodehouse | *Mulliner Nights* |
| ROLLO | Pym | *An Academic Question* |
| RUPERT | Wodehouse | *Lord Emsworth and Others* |
| SACHEVERELL | Wodehouse | *Mulliner Nights* |
| SAMSON | Waugh | *Black Mischief* |
| SEBASTIAN | Waugh | *Brideshead Revisited* |
| SEBASTIEN | Waugh | *Decline and Fall* |
| TYRELL | Pym | *Excellent Women* |
| WADSWORTH | Wodehouse | *Lord Emsworth and Others* |
| WILMOT | Wodehouse | *Lord Emsworth and Others* |

---

This may have accounted for Emma's christian name, for it had seemed to Beatrix unfair to call her daughter Emily, a name associated with her grandmother's servants rather than the author of *Wuthering Heights,* so Emma had been chosen, perhaps with the hope that some of the qualities possessed by the heroine of the novel might be perpetrated.

—Barbara Pym, *A Few Green Leaves*

**Lord Byron's Daughter** × **Two**

Winifred came up to me, her eyes shining. 'Oh, Mildred,' she breathed, '*what* do you think her name is?'

I said I had no idea.

'Allegra!' she told me. 'Isn't that lovely? Allegra Gray.'

I found myself wondering if it was really Mrs. Gray's name, or if she had perhaps adopted it instead of a more conventional and uninteresting one. 'Wasn't Allegra the name of Byron's natural daughter?' I asked.

'Byron! How splendid!' Winifred clasped her hands in rapture.

—Barbara Pym, *Excellent Women*

"What's her name?"

"Allegra. Like Lord Byron's daughter."

. . . "I should never dare to give a name like that to a child. It is too much of a challenge," Robert said. "She would be almost sure to grow up fat and flat-footed and terribly Andante."

—Elizabeth Taylor, *A View of the Harbour*

# ORIGINALS

The British are responsible for the invention of the steam engine, the vacuum cleaner, the flush toilet—and the name Wendy. For centuries now, when British poets and novelists could not withdraw the appropriate (usually female) name from the national name bank, they simply concocted their own. Some of their more felicitous creations:

*Estella:* Introduced by Charles Dickens in *Great Expectations* for the ward of Miss Haversham, 1861.

*Geraldine:* First used by the sixteenth-century Romantic poet the Earl of Surrey, who dedicated many of his love poems to "the fair Geraldine"—actually his amorata, Lady Elizabeth Fitzgerald. Geraldine literally means "one of the Fitzgeralds."

*Imogen:* When the manuscript of Shakespeare's play

*Cymbeline* was transcribed, the name of the romantic character Innogen was misspelled as Imogen.

*Lorna:* Name created by R. D. Blackmore for the heroine of his novel, *Lorna Doone,* in 1869, probably inspired by the Scottish place name Lorn.

*Malvina:* Invented by the eighteenth-century poet James Macpherson for his Ossianic poems.

*Miranda:* Name coined by Shakespeare for the heroine of his comedy *The Tempest.*

*Myra:* Contributed by the poet Fulke Greville (1554–1628) in a series of love poems—possibly as an anagram of Mary.

*Pamela:* First used by Sir Philip Sidney in his sixteenth-century pastoral epic, *Arcadia,* where the emphasis was on the second syllable.

*Perdita:* A Shakespearean invention for *The Winter's Tale,* and a fitting appellation for an abandoned baby princess.

*Stella:* Another Sir Philip Sidney coinage, this one was for his famous series of sonnets called *Astrophel to Stella,* inspired by his beloved Lady Penelope Devereux.

*Vanessa:* Created by Jonathan Swift for his poem *Cadenus and Vanessa,* 1713, dedicated to his young love Esther Vanhomrigh. It combined the first syllable of her surname with a pet form of Esther.

*Wendy:* A name invented not by but for James M. Barrie,

by a young friend named Margaret Henley. It is assumed to have evolved from her childish pronunciation of the word *fwend,* which led to the nickname Fwendy-Wendy. Barrie introduced it to the world at large in *Peter Pan* in 1904.

Most of these names were created for beloved females, but we have come up with one male name, although it might not necessarily be your favorite:

*Cedric* was the invention of Sir Walter Scott for his novel *Ivanhoe.* It was based either on the Celtic word *cedrych* or on the Old English name Ceredig.

# $E_T$ ALIA

There have been other memorable and adoptable names sprinkled through the history of Brit Lit, and here is a sampling of those associated with particular writers of poetry and fiction:

## F E M A L E

| | |
|---|---|
| ABIGAIL .......... | Beaumont and Fletcher |
| ADA .............. | Lord Byron |
| ADELINE .......... | Lord Byron |
| ALICE ............. | Lewis Carroll |
| AMANDA ......... | Noel Coward |
| AMELIA .......... | Henry Fielding |
| BELINDA .......... | Alexander Pope |
| BRIDGET .......... | Henry Fielding |
| CANDIDA ......... | George Bernard Shaw |
| CHRISTABEL ....... | Samuel Taylor Coleridge |
| CLARISSA ......... | Samuel Richardson |
| DAHLIA ........... | George Meredith |

DEBRAH .......... Henry Fielding
DINAH ............ Laurence Sterne
ELIZA ............. George Bernard Shaw
EUSTACIA ........ Thomas Hardy
FLEUR ............ John Galsworthy
GLORIANA ........ Edmund Spenser
GUDRUN .......... D. H. Lawrence
HOLLY ............ John Galsworthy
JEMIMA ........... Beatrix Potter
JUSTINE ........... Lawrence Durrell
LEILA ............. Lord Byron
MAUD ............ Alfred, Lord Tennyson
MOLLY ........... Henry Fielding
PAMELA .......... Samuel Richardson
PIPPA ............ Robert Browning
RHODA ........... George Meredith
RIMA ............. W. H. Hudson
ROMOLA .......... George Eliot
ROWENA .......... Sir Walter Scott
SHIRLEY .......... Charlotte Brontë
SOPHIA ........... Henry Fielding
SUSANNAH ....... Laurence Sterne
TESS ............. Thomas Hardy
THOMASIN ........ Thomas Hardy
UNA .............. Edmund Spenser
URSULA .......... D. H. Lawrence
VELVET .......... Enid Bagnold
ZULEIKA .......... Sir Max Beerbohm

## M  A  L  E

ANGEL ............ Thomas Hardy
BEVIS ............. Richard Jefferies
CASMILUS ........ Stevie Smith
DORIAN .......... Oscar Wilde
GARETH .......... Alfred, Lord Tennyson

GULLY . . . . . . . . . . . . . Joyce Cary
HUMPHREY . . . . . . . . Tobias Smollett
JOLYON . . . . . . . . . . . . John Galsworthy
JUDE . . . . . . . . . . . . . . Thomas Hardy
KIM . . . . . . . . . . . . . . . Rudyard Kipling
LEMUEL . . . . . . . . . . . Jonathan Swift
NICOL . . . . . . . . . . . . . Sir Walter Scott
OBADIAH . . . . . . . . . . Anthony Trollope
ORLANDO . . . . . . . . . Virginia Woolf
PEREGRINE . . . . . . . . . Tobias Smollett
QUENTIN . . . . . . . . . . Sir Walter Scott
SILAS . . . . . . . . . . . . . . George Eliot
SOAMES . . . . . . . . . . . John Galsworthy
TRISTRAM . . . . . . . . . Laurence Sterne

---

"Must a name mean something?" Alice asked doubtfully.

"Of course it must," Humpty Dumpty said with a short laugh:

"My name means the shape I am—and a good handsome shape it is too. With a name like yours, you might be any shape, almost."

—Lewis Carroll, *Alice's Adventures in Wonderland*

GWENDOLEN: . . . my ideal has always been to love some one of the name of Ernest. There is something in that name that inspires absolute confidence. . . . It is a divine name. It has music of its own. It produces vibrations.

JACK: Well, really, Gwendolen, I must say that I think there are lots of other much nicer names. I think Jack, for instance, a charming name.

GWENDOLEN: Jack? . . . No, there is very little music in the name Jack. . . . It does not thrill. It produces absolutely no vibrations. . . . I have known several Jacks, and they all, without exception, were more than usually plain. Besides, Jack is a notorious domesticity for John! And I pity any woman who is married to a man called John. She would probably never be allowed to know the entrancing pleasure of a single moment's solitude. The only really safe name is Ernest.

—Oscar Wilde, *The Importance of Being Earnest*

If you should have a boy, do not christen him John, and persuade George not to let his partiality for me come across. 'Tis a bad name and goes against a man. If my name had been Edmund, I should have been more fortunate.

—John Keats, in a letter to his sister-in-law, 1820

[SHE:] . . . my silly, unhappy name. Oh, if only I had been christened Mary Jane, or Gladys Muriel, or Beatrice, or Francesca, or Guinevere, or something quite common! But Aurora! Aurora! I'm the only Aurora in London; and everybody knows it. I believe I'm the only Aurora in the world.

—George Bernard Shaw, *How He Lied to Her Husband*

My advice to everyone is to change their name at once if they're the least unhappy with their lives. In Utopia everyone will choose a new name at seven, at eleven, at sixteen and twenty-four. And naturally women at forty-five, or when the last child has grown up and left home, whichever is the earliest. . . . Then life will be seen to start over, not finish. . . . But so many of us, either feeling our identities to be fragile, or out of misplaced loyalty to our parents, feel we must stick with the names we start out with. The given name is a dead giveaway of our parents' ambition for us—whether to diminish or enhance, ignore us as much as possible or control us forever.

—Fay Weldon, *Darcy's Utopia*

# THERE'LL ALWAYS BE AN ENGLAND

# Normans, is that You?

## Or a Brief History of English Naming

So, where did all these names come from?

The history of British nomenclature, not surprisingly, reflects the culturally convoluted history of the country. Its Celtic roots remain visible in the form of Irish and Scottish names. Of the invaders who followed in historical times, only the Romans failed to leave a direct mark (though poets inspired by the classical era—see page 68—and earnest Victorian and dreamy pre-Raphaelite parents would later make up for this). Anglo-Saxon colonizers did bring with them a few still-feasible Germanic names, such as Edward (originally Eadward) and Alfred (Aelfred), but a great many more were of the far clunkier Aethel family (at first only borne by the younger sons of the hereditary kings or earls), such as Aethelwulf and Aethelstan. A small number of names derived from Old English, such as Edwin and Audrey, were revived during the Victorian period. In all these cases—Old German, Old English, Gothic, and Old Scandinavian—each individual bore a single name, which was usually made up of two elements taken from a stock of special name-making words.

The Norman Conquest of 1066 changed all this. Within a couple of generations, first the Anglo-Saxon nobles and then the peasantry dropped the Old English names, until they had completely disappeared, to be replaced by Gallicized forms of Teutonic and Norse names, including such standards as the following:

| | |
|---|---|
| GEOFFREY | ROGER |
| HUGH | WALTER |
| RICHARD | WILLIAM |
| ROBERT | |

At the same time, the Breton knights who rode with the Normans helped popularize names such as Alan and Sampson.

The rising power of the medieval Catholic Church had a considerable effect on naming, since it decreed that babies could be baptized only with names borne by some holy Christian, thus encompassing a long list of saints and martyrs, including Matthew, John, Peter, Andrew, Thomas, Philip, Catherine, Agnes, and Margaret, while the rediscovery of the classical world in the late twelfth and early thirteenth centuries led to a fashion for Latinate forms, such as Norma, Cassandra, and Camilla. Children born on or near major feast days were sometimes named accordingly—giving us the origins of Noel, Natalie, and even Tiffany. Another reversal came with the Reformation: Since the Protestants despised everything connected with Catholic dogma and ceremony, the use of saints' names, except for those of the Apostles, was renounced. In their place, Old Testament names—rarely used at that time with any frequency—returned with a vengeance, and Hebrew names like Sarah, Aaron, Gideon,

Joshua, Moses, and Nathaniel became popular. Puritan extremists sought obscure names in the Bible (Zaphnath) and went so far as to coin their own names, such as Praise-God and The Lord Is Near.

The Counter-Reformation found aristocratic family names such as Sydney, Percy, Clive, Cecil, Neville, and Howard being used as Christian names. The monarchy always had a strong influence on British nomenclature (see page 10): the long-reigning Elizabeth I's power is still felt, and the ascension of the Georges to the throne brought in a new Teutonic strain, with names like Charlotte, Wilhelmina, Caroline, Carl, Ernest, and Frederick.

From the eighteenth century on, the pot has been sweetened and spiced by any number of influences leading to a contemporary eclecticism inconceivable a few centuries ago, when 62.5 percent of the British male population was named either William, John, or Thomas.

# A GIRL NAMED BASIL

From the thirteenth through the fifteenth centuries, it was common practice for girls in Britain to be given masculine names, according to E. G. Withycombe, the original author of the *Oxford Dictionary of English Christian Names*. Nicholas, for instance, was such a popular girls' name in Scotland that it continued to be used there until the end of the seventeenth century. Other male names normally given to girls in Olde England include:

| | |
|---|---|
| ALEXANDER | GILBERT |
| AUBREY | GILES |
| BASIL | JAMES |
| DOUGLAS | PHILIP |
| EDMUND | REYNOLD |
| EUSTACE | SIMON |

Girls' names that previously belonged to boys include:

CRYSTAL

ESMÉ

EVELYN

FLORENCE

JOCELYN

# THE
# QUINTESSENTIALS

**T**here is a large body of British nomenclature consisting of names rarely heard in the United States. Names that conjure up high tea, Harrods, porcelain complexions, and polo. Not that they're necessarily upper class (see the Social Standing chapter, page 45), they just sound that way to the American ear. These quintessential British names are:

## G I R L S

| | |
|---|---|
| AGATHA | ANONA |
| ALLEGRA | ANTHEA |
| ALTHEA | APHRA |
| AMABEL | ARABELLA |
| AMINTA | ARAMINTA |
| ANGELICA | AUGUSTA |
| ANNABEL | AVIS/AVICE |

AVRIL
BEATA
BEATRIX
BERYL
BRYONY
CANDIDA
CASSANDRA
CATRIONA
CECILIA
CECILY
CHARMIAN
CHRISTABEL
CICELY
CLARICE
CLARINDA
CLARISSA
CLELIA
CLEMENTINE
CORDELIA
CORINNE
CRESSIDA
DAHLIA
DAPHNE
DAVINA
DILYS
DOMENICA
DORCAS
DORINDA
DRUSILLA
DULCIE
EDWINA
EMMELINE
ENA

ESTELLA
ESTRELLA
EUGENIE
EVANGELINE
FELICIA
FELICITY
FENELLA
FEODORA
FIONA
FLAVIA
FLORA
GEMMA
GEORGIANA
GEORGINA
GERMAINE
GILLIAN/JILLIAN
GRANIA
GWENDOLINE
HELENA
HERMIONE
HONOR
HONORIA
IMOGEN
INDIA
IOLE
IONA
IONE
IVY
JACOBA
JACQUETTA
JADE
JEMIMA
JEMMA

JENNA
JESSAMINE/ JES-
  SAMYN/ JESSAMY
JOCASTA
JOCELYN
KERENZA
KERSTIE
LARISSA
LAVINIA
LESLEY
LETITIA
LETTICE
LIVIA
LOUISA
LUCINDA
LUCRETIA
LYNSEY
MAGDALEN
MALVINA
MARCELLA
MARIAH
MARIBEL
MARIBELLA
MARIETTA
MARIGOLD
MARINA
MATILDA
MAVIS
MIRABEL/
  MIRABELLE
NERISSA
NESSA

NICOLA
NICOLETTE
OCTAVIA
OPAL
OPHELIA
OTTILIE
OTTOLINE
PANDORA
PANSY
PENELOPE
PERDITA
PERSIS
PETA
PETRONELLA
PETULA
PHILIPPA
PHILLIDA
PHILOMENA
PIPPA
POPPY
PORTIA
POSY
PRIMROSE
PRISCILLA
PRUDENCE
PRUNELLA
RAINA
REINE
ROBINA
ROSALIND
ROSAMUND
ROWENA

The British don't like 'Junr' [sic] after a name (and never call their offspring Junior except in trans-Atlantic parody) and they don't let strings of fathers and sons be called I, II, III, etc. . . . a distinction that we keep for monarchs.

—Basil Cottle, *Names*

| | |
|---|---|
| ROXANA | UNITY |
| SABINA | URSULA |
| SELINA | VENETIA |
| SERAPHINA | VERONICA |
| SERENA | VIOLA |
| SIDONY | VIOLET |
| TAMSIN | WINIFRED |
| TEAL | ZANDRA |
| TEODORA/ | ZARA |
| THEODORA | ZENOBIA |
| UNA | ZULEIKA |

## B O Y S

| | |
|---|---|
| ADRIAN | ANTONY |
| ALARIC | ARCHIBALD |
| ALDOUS | AUBERON |
| ALEC | AUBREY |
| ALISTAIR | AUGUSTINE |
| AMBROSE | BAILEY |

BALTHAZAR
BARNABUS
BARTHOLOMEW
BASIL
BENEDICT
BEVIS
CECIL
CEDRIC
CLEMENT
CLIVE
COLIN
CORIN
CRISPIN
CYRIL
DAMIAN
DARBY
DENHOLM
DENIS
DERMOT
DERRY
DESMOND
DIGBY
DORIAN
DROGO
DUDLEY
DUNCAN
DUNSTAN
EBENEZER
EUSTACE
EVELYN
EVERARD
EWAN
FABIAN

FELIX
GARETH
GILES
GRAHAM
GUY
HORATIO
HUGH
HUGO
HUMPHREY
INGRAM
INIGO
IVO
IVOR
JAGO
JASPER
JOCELYN
KENELM
LACHLAN
LAMBERT
LANCELOT
LEANDER
LESLIE
LUCIEN
LUCIUS
MALCOLM
MARCUS
MONTAGUE
MORLEY
NEVILLE
NIGEL
NINIAN
NORRIS
ORIN/ORRIN

| | |
|---|---|
| ORLANDO | RUPERT |
| PERCY | SACHEVERELL |
| PEREGRINE | SEPTIMUS |
| PHILO | SHERIDAN |
| PIERS | ST. JOHN (pronounced |
| REDMOND | "Sinjin") |
| REGINALD | TARQUIN |
| REX | TOBY |
| ROBIN | TORQUIL |
| RODERICK | TRISTAN |
| RODNEY | TRISTRAM |
| ROLAND | URIAH |
| ROLF | VERE |
| ROLLIN | VIVIAN |
| ROLLO | WYNDHAM |
| ROWAN | |

Then there is another group, names that are used in this country but nowhere to the degree that they are in the UK. Charlotte, for example, which is just beginning to come back in America after a century's hiatus, is #1 on the Brit Hit Parade (see page 10). Some, like Henrietta and Ralph, may have to wait a bit longer. Others—such as Simon and Susannah, Oliver and Olivia—have become fully assimilated, yet still retain that quintessential British ring.

## G I R L S

| | |
|---|---|
| ALICE | BEATRICE |
| ANGELA | CELIA |
| ANTONIA | CHARLOTTE |

CLAIRE
DELIA
ELEANOR
ELIZA
EMMA
FRANCESCA
HARRIET
HELEN
HENRIETTA
HILARY
ISABEL
JULIET
KAY
LOUISE

LUCY
MAUD
MONICA
NATALIE
OLIVIA
PAMELA
PAULINE
SOPHIA
SOPHIE
SUSANNAH
VALERIE
VANESSA
VICTORIA

## B O Y S

BARNABY
DEREK
DOMINIC
GEOFFREY
GREGORY
IAN
JARED
JULIAN

JUSTIN
NOEL
OLIVER
RALPH
SEBASTIAN
SIMON
SPENCER
TREVOR

### We Say Soph-ee-a, They Say Soph-eye-a

The British, as all Americans know, pronounce their words funny. They say "cahn't" and "dahnce" and "Frahnce." And they also pronounce some names differently than Americans do: Sophia, for instance, is often "Soph-eye-a"; Clementine is pronounced "Clementeen"; the first "a" in Georgiana is a long one; and Isaiah is "Eye-zeye-uh."

Then there is the case of Colin, recently brought to the forefront by the renown of Gen. Colin ("KOH-lin") Powell and the subject of an "On Language" column by William Safire in the *New York Times* (March 17, 1991). In Britain, the name is always pronounced "KAH-lin," which is also the preferred pronunciation in *Random House Dictionary II*. But an American World War II hero named Colin P. Kelly, Jr., led to a rash of namesakes pronounced "KOH-lin," one of whom is General Powell. How does he feel about the pronunciation of his name? As he told an interviewer quoted by Safire: "My parents named me KAH-lin. . . . [They] were British subjects and they knew how the name should be pronounced." With the fame of KOH-lin Kelly, "[M]y friends in the street . . . started calling me KOH-lin."

According to Safire, the General is comfortable with both pronunciations but prefers KOH-lin, "much to the regret of my British friends, who consider us a bunch of ignorant Americans for mispronouncing the name."

# TRANSATLANTIC TRAVELERS

**W**hy is it that Americans are familiar with the Scottish name Sheena and not Seona? Very often it's because of a single transporter, someone famous enough to make the name known to the American ear. Some of these names have achieved widespread popularity, while others have seen only occasional use. The British, Scottish, and Welsh Names with these names include:

## F E M A L E

| | |
|---|---|
| CILLA | Black |
| GLYNIS | John |
| GREER | Garson |
| HAYLEY | Mills |
| HERMIONE | Gingold |
| HONOR | Blackman |

**No Troys, Please, We're British**

Britons haven't taken to Dwight or Calvin (never having had presidents with these first names), or to Irving, or to Bradley and Ashley in the latest Australian list, and discriminating minds have rebuffed . . . Craig, Shane, Damian, Dean, Leigh, Troy, Dale, Kane, and other Australian favourites.

American names are often envied and borrowed, though nice insular Britons feel a strong resentment at the arrival of meaningless things like Darren and ignore them; but the general public lap them up.

—Basil Cottle, *Names*

MOIRA . . . . . . . . . . . . . Shearer
PETULA . . . . . . . . . . . Clark
PIPPA . . . . . . . . . . . . . Scott
PRUNELLA . . . . . . . . Scales
SHEENA . . . . . . . . . . . Easton

## M  A  L  E

ALDOUS . . . . . . . . . . . Huxley
ALISTAIR . . . . . . . . . . Cooke
AUBERON . . . . . . . . . Waugh
(C.) AUBREY . . . . . . . . Smith
BASIL . . . . . . . . . . . . . Rathbone

CEDRIC ............ Hardwicke
CLIVE .............. Brook
DENHOLM ......... Elliot
DUDLEY ........... Moore
DYLAN ............. Thomas
EMLYN ............. Williams
ERROL ............. Flynn
KINGSLEY .......... Amis
LESLIE ............. Howard
NEVILLE ........... Chamberlain
NICOL ............. Williamson
NIGEL .............. Bruce
NOEL .............. Coward
REX ............... Harrison
TREVOR ........... Howard
WINSTON .......... Churchill

# Names
# Geographica

The map of England provides an interesting roster of territorial names. Some (Devon, Chester, Clifford) have already segued into personal nomenclature; others are there for the taking. Some sound decidedly male, but many can be used for either sex.

ALTON
ARLEY
ARRAM
ASHBY
BARCLAY
BARNARD
BARTON
BEVERLEY
BLYTH
BOSTON
BRADFORD

BRANDON
BRISCOE
BRISTOL
BURGESS
CALLINGTON
CARLTON
CARLYLE
CHELSEA
CHESTER
CLEE
CLIFFORD

| | |
|---|---|
| CLIFTON | MITCHAM |
| CROSBY | MONTGOMERY |
| DALTON | MORLEY |
| DEVON | NELSON |
| DORSET | NORTON |
| ELY | OTLEY |
| GUERNSEY | PRESTON |
| HARRINGTON | RAMSEY |
| JARROW | REETH |
| JERSEY | RICHMOND |
| KEIGHLEY | ROYSTON |
| KENDAL | SEATON |
| KENT | SPALDING |
| LEIGH | STRATTON |
| LEIGHTON | SUTTON |
| LEYLAND | THORNE |
| LINCOLN | WALTON |
| LINDSEY | WESTON |
| MARLOW | WINSLOW |
| MILTON | |

---

MRS DUBEDAT: My name is Jennifer.

RIDGEON: A strange name.

MRS DUBEDAT: Not in Cornwall. I am Cornish. It's only what you call Guinevere.

RIDGEON: [repeating the names with a certain pleasure in them] Guinevere. Jennifer.

—George Bernard Shaw, *The Doctor's Dilemma*

# A DIVERSITY OF DIMINUTIVES

You'll find almost as many Christophers called Kit as Chris in Kent, more Wills than Bills in Wessex, and Jamies as plentiful as Jimmys in Poole. In a country where at one time 57 percent of the female population bore only three names (Mary, Anne, and Elizabeth) and it was not uncommon to give more than one child in a family the same name, it's no wonder that a wild diversity of diminutives and pet names sprang up, many of which did not ever migrate to the New World. *The Oxford Dictionary of English Christian Names,* for example, cites nine different nicknames for Bartholomew (not even including the expected Bart)—Bat, Bate, Batty, Bartie, Bartelet, Bartelot, Batcock, Batkin, and Tolly.

The British devised several different routes for arriving at nicknames. The most obvious was the shortening of a name (William = Will, Katherine = Kat), which gave rise to rhyming forms (Will/Bill, Rob/Bob). Unfortunately, some of the more colorful of these have died out, like Dob, Hob, and Nob for Robert. A variety of diminutive suffixes were also ap-

She was called in the Institution Harriet Beadle—
an arbitrary name, of course. Now Harriet we
changed into Hatty, and then into Tatty, because
as practical people, we thought even a playful
name might be a new thing to her, and might have
a softening and affectionate kind of effect.

—Charles Dickens, *Little Dorrit*

'Do you like the name of Nicodemus? Think it over.
Nick, or Noddy.'

. . . 'It is not a name as I could wish any one that
I had a respect for, to call *me* by; but there may be
persons that would not view it with the same objec-
tions. . . .

. . . 'Noddy. That's my name. Noddy—or Nick—
Boffin . . .'

—Charles Dickens, *Our Mutual Friend*

plied—*et, ot, in, on, kin* and *cock*—not just the ubiquitous
y and *ie* we use in this country.

On the other side of the coin, nicknames are rarely used
as full-fledged names in the UK—you won't find many Sams
or Alexes on British birth certificates. And—a practice being
picked up by their American cousins—the Brits do tend to

call their children by their full given names. In Holland Park, you would be much more likely to hear "Charles" or "Katharine" called out than "Charlie" (forget Chuck) or "Kathy."

What follows is a list of some of the British pet names rarely used in America, so that even if you pick one of the classics, you can call your child something distinctive:

## G I R L S

| | |
|---|---|
| ALEXANDRA | ZAN |
| AMANDA | MANDA |
| BARBARA | BOBS, BAB, BABBIE, BARRA |
| BEATRICE | BEAT, BEAH |
| BRIDGET | BRIDIE |
| CAMILLA | CAM |
| CAROLINE | CARO |
| CATHERINE | CATTIE |
| CHARLOTTE | LOTTA, TOTTIE, CHARTY |
| CYNTHIA | CINDA |
| DEBORAH | DEBS, DEBO |
| DOROTHY | DORO |
| ELEANOR | NELL |
| ELIZABETH | BAB, BETTA, LETTY, TETTY, TIBBY, LILIBET (the Queen's childhood name) |
| FIONA | FEE |
| FLORENCE | FLORY, FLOSS |
| GWENDOLYN | GWENDA, WYN |
| HARRIET | HARRI, HATTIE, HATSY, HETTY |
| IMOGEN | IMMY |
| ISABEL | IBBY, IB, TIBBY |
| JOSEPHINE | FEENY |
| KATHARINE | KAT, KATH, KITTY |
| LOUISE | LU, LULU |
| MARGARET | MAG, MEGGIE, MAGO |

| | |
|---|---|
| MARY .............. | MOLL, POLLY, MOLLY |
| MELANIE ........... | MELLY |
| MELISSA .......... | LISSA |
| OLIVIA ............ | LIVIA, LIVVY |
| PAMELA .......... | PAMMY |
| PATRICIA ......... | PATIA |
| PHILIPPA .......... | FLIPPA, PIP, PIPPA |
| SUSAN ............ | SUKIE |
| VANESSA .......... | NESSA, VAN, VANIA, VANNY |
| VERONICA ......... | VONNY |
| VICTORIA ......... | TORY |
| VIRGINIA ......... | VIRGIE |

## B O Y S

| | |
|---|---|
| ABRAHAM ......... | BRAM |
| ANDREW .......... | TANDY |
| BENJAMIN ......... | BENNO |
| CHARLES ......... | CHAS/CHAZ, CHAD, CHAR, CHICO, CARLO |
| CHRISTOPHER ...... | KIT, CHRISTY |
| DESMOND ........ | DESI, DEZI |
| DUNCAN ......... | DUNN |
| EDWARD .......... | NED |
| GARY ............. | GAZ |
| GERALD .......... | GED |
| GILBERT .......... | GIB, GIBBY |
| GORDON ......... | GORE |
| GRAHAM ......... | GRAM |
| JAMES ............ | JAM, JIMBO |
| JEREMY ........... | JEM |
| JOHN ............. | JOCK, JOCKO |
| LAURENCE ........ | LAURIE, LAURO |
| PHILIP ............ | PIP |
| RALPH ............ | RAFE, RAFF |

RICHARD .......... DIX, DIXY
ROBERT ............ ROBIN
SEBASTIAN ......... SEB
SIMON ............. SIMS
THEODORE ........ TAD, TADDEO, TELLY
THOMAS ........... MASO, TIP
WILLIAM .......... WILLS

# SCOTTISH
# NAMES

**W**hat's a Scottish name? you may be wondering. Bonnie? Not really. In fact, by and large, the Scots use the same names that the English do. There are, however, some differences. For one, the Scots use some of these names with much greater frequency: Archie, for instance, and Agnes and Janet and Margaret. For another, surnames (often the mother's maiden name) and place names are bestowed on babies more often in Scotland than in its more proper southerly neighbor. The Scots have also adopted, with fervor, the British penchant for giving girls feminized versions of male names. And then there are the "real" Gaelic Scottish names, familiar ones like Angus and Duncan and Fiona, as well as more exotic variations such as Ailsa and Shona and Mungo—with nary a Bonnie among them.

Here are names both familiar and un that are well-used in Scotland:

## G I R L S

### F A M I L I A R

| | |
|---|---|
| AGNES | JEAN |
| ALISON | JENNIFER |
| ANNABEL | JESSIE (diminutive of |
| ANNABELLA | Janet) |
| AVRIL | KIRSTIE |
| BEATRIX | LAURA |
| CLEMENTINE | LAURIE |
| EMMA | LESLEY |
| FIONA | LORNA |
| FLORA | MAGGIE |
| GEORGINA | MAISIE |
| GLEN(N) | MARGARET |
| GRACE | MAY |
| HEATHER | MYRA |
| INA | SHEENA |
| ISOBEL | STEPHANIE |
| JANET | THOMASINA |

### L E S S   F A M I L I A R

| | |
|---|---|
| AILI | ANNOR |
| AILSA | ANNOT |
| AINSLIE | BARABALL |
| ALEXINA | BEATHAG/BETHOC |
| ANGUSINA | BETHIA |

CAIRISTONA
CATRIONA
CHRISSELLE
DAVIDA
DAVINA
EDINA
EILIDH
ELSPETH
EUPHEMIA
FENELLA
FRANCA
FRANCINA
GINEVRA
GLYNIS
INNIS
IONA
IONE
ISHBEL
ISLA
ISMAY
JACOBINA

JAMESINA
LENNOX
LILIAS/LILIES
LORN(E)
MAIRI
MOIRA/MOIRE
MORAG
MORNA
MORVEN
NESSIE
OSLA
ROBENA
ROVENA
SENGA
SEONA
SHONA(H)
SINNIE
SIUSAN
SORCHA
THORA

# B O Y S

# F A M I L I A R

ANDREW
ANGUS
ARCHIBALD
BLAIR

BOYD
BRUCE
CAMERON
CAMPBELL

CHRISTIE
CHRISTOPHER
CRAIG
DALLAS
DAVID
DONALD
DOUGLAS
DUNCAN
FRASER
GAVIN
GILES
GORDON
GRAHAM
GRANT
HAMILTON
HOUSTON
HUGH
HUNTER
IAN
IVOR
KEITH
KENNETH
KIRK
KYLE

LESLIE
LOGAN
LORNE
LYLE
MACDONALD
MALCOLM
MAXWELL
MORRISON
MURRAY
MYLES
NEIL
NEVIL(LE)
PRESTON
QUINTON
RAMSAY
RODERICK
ROSS
SCOTT
SINCLAIR
STEWART
TODD
WALLACE
WILSON

## L E S S   F A M I L I A R

ADAIR
AED(H)
AENEAS
AINDREAS

ALASDAIR
ARRAN
AULAY
BAIRD

BALFOUR
BARTHRAM
BEATHAN
BIRK
BRAN
BUSBY
CAIRNS
CALLUM
CAMDEN
CARMICHAEL
CATHAL
CRAWFORD
CRIGHTON
CUTHBERT
DENHOLM
DIARMID
DRUMMOND
DUGAL(D)
EACHANN/
   EACHUNN
ERSKINE
EWAN/EWEN/EUAN
FARQUHAR
FERGUS
FIFE/FYFE
FINLAY
FORBES
GEORDIE
GILCHRIST
GILLANDERS
GILLIAN
GLEANN
GLENDON

GREGOR
HABERT
HAMISH
IAIN/IAIAN
INNES
JOCK
KEDDY
KEIR
KELVIN
KENTIGERN
KERR
LACHLAN
LAIRD
LAWREN
LEITH
LENNOX
LUCAIS
MACDOUGAL
MAGNUS
MICHEIL
MORRICE
MUIR
MUNGO
MURDO
MURDOCH
NIALL
NINIAN
PADRUIG
PARLAN
PEADAIR
SEUMAS
SIM
STEAPHAN

STRUAN            TURVAL
TAVIS             UILLEAM/UILLIAM
TORQUIL

---

**In Scotland, These Names Are Selling Like Shortbread**

The most popular names in Scotland are also well used by American parents and throughout the British Isles. Scotland's most recent Top Five list does, however, present its own idiosyncratic configuration: Only the number-one girls' name, Emma, appears on the British Top Ten, and none of the most popular Scottish boys' names is as widely used in England. There's more crossover with American name popularity lists: Scottish stars Sarah, Stephanie, Christopher, Andrew, and David are all featured on America's Top Ten. One major difference between Scotland and the United States: the name Jason, long an American favorite, just made the Scottish Top 100 for the very first time.

For 1990, the five most popular names for each sex in Scotland were:

Girls                   Boys

1. EMMA                 1. DAVID
2. LAURA                2. CHRISTOPHER
3. SARAH                3. CRAIG
4. STEPHANIE            4. SCOTT
5. KIRSTIE              5. ANDREW

# WELSH NAMES

Many Welsh names are—let's be frank (or, as the Welsh might say, ffranck)—very weird. The Welsh language itself is weird. If you want to go to a place called Glyndyfrdwy, for instance, or Llanymawddwy, how exactly are you going to ask for directions? Likewise, if you name your child Brycheiniog or Lleucu, how are you going to call him (or, in the case of Lleucu, her) to dinner?

Of course, not all Welsh names are so strange. A few, notably Gwen, Morgan, Dylan, Owen, and even the ubiquitous Jennifer, have established themselves in the world at large. But there are dozens and dozens and dozens of other names that, while used in Wales itself, have not moved far beyond Cardiff or Llandudno. One reason there are so many Welsh names—and more to the point, so many bizarre ones—is that the Welsh used no surnames at all until the Reformation, and even then, have stuck to a few common favorites, such as Jones and Thomas. The wide range of unusual first names was the only way to distinguish one person from another.

The origins of Welsh names reflect the diverse groups of invaders that swept through Britain at various times in history. The oldest Welsh names have a Celtic base: Rhys, for instance, and Llywely, and Hywel. Others, such as Emlys and Padarn, are Latin in origin. Still others are Welsh variations of Norman names: Rhisiart for Richard, Gwilym for William. The Welsh also commonly adopt place names and nature words (Gwanwen, for instance, means spring) as first names.

For those with ties to this beautiful corner of Britain, or for parents in search of an established yet highly original name, the Welsh roster provides fertile hunting ground. Many of the girls' names, in particular, are lovely—the wide range of names with the traditional feminine *-wen* ending (*-wyn* is male)—from the familiar Bronwen to the more exotic Alwen, Anwen, Bradwen, Collwen, Elwen, ad infinitum—are notable, as are Welsh forms of familiar names, such as Alys, Catrin, Elan, and Marged. Rhiannon is a personal favorite now enjoying wider use throughout Britain.

A note on how, if you choose a Welsh name, you are going to call your child to dinner. *A, e, i, o,* and *u,* when standing alone, are usually what we called in school short vowels, pronounced as in "pat," "bet," "bit," "pot," and "but." *Y* is pronounced as the short *i* ("bit"); *ae* is pronounced as *ee.* C and *g* are both hard, as in "cake" and "gate." Now for the tough part: *ch* is a guttural sound, as in "Bach," *dd* is pronounced as *th,* and in *rh* the *h* is silent. *Ph* is pronounced as *f, f* is pronounced as *v,* and *ff* is pronounced as *f.* And the infamous *Ll?* Just pretend there's only one. Go figure. To begin with, here's a short list of user-friendly, sometimes modernized, but basically Welsh names:

## G I R L S

| | |
|---|---|
| ALMIDA | GWYNNE |
| BRONWEN | ISOLDE |
| BRYN | MARIEL |
| CORDELIA | MEREDITH |
| ENID | RHONWYN |
| GLADYS | ROWENA |
| GLENDA | SIAN |
| GLYNIS | VANORA |
| GUINEVERE | WINIFRED |
| GWENDOLYN | WYNN/WYNNE |
| GWYNETH | |

## B O Y S

| | |
|---|---|
| ARTHUR | GLENN |
| BEVAN | GOWER |
| BRICE | GRIFFIN |
| CAI | GRIFFITH |
| CAREY | GWYN |
| CARSON | HOWELL |
| CLYDE | KENT |
| DEWEY | KIMBALL |
| DREW | LINCOLN |
| DYLAN | LLEWELYN |
| EBEN | LLOYD |
| EVAN | MORGAN |
| GARETH | OWEN |
| GARTH | PARRY |
| GAVIN | POWELL |

RHYS/REECE/REESE    TRISTRAM
SAYER    VAUGHN
TAFFY    WYN/WYNNE
TRISTAN

And now, a wider selection of Welsh names—and this isn't even close to all of them—in their strange and varied splendor:

## G I R L S

| | |
|---|---|
| ADWEN | BRANWEN |
| AERES | BRIALLEN |
| AERFEN | BRONMAI |
| AERONWEN | BRYTHONWEN |
| ALDYTH | CADI/CATI |
| ALWEN | CAIN |
| ALYS | CARI |
| ANEIRA | CARWEN |
| ANONA | CARYS |
| ANWEN | CATRIN |
| ANWYL | CEINWEN |
| ARANWEN | CERIAN |
| ARIANNELL | CERIDWEN |
| ARIANWEN | CERYS |
| ARWEN | COLLWEN |
| ARWENNA | CRISIANT |
| BETHAN | CYFFIN |
| BETRYS | DARON |
| BRADWEN | DELWEN |
| BRANGWEN | DELYTH |

DERWENA
DERYN
DILWEN
DILYS
DU
DWYNWEN
DWYSAN
EIDDWEN
EILWEN
EIRA
EIRIAN
EIRWEN
EIRYS
ELAN/ELEN
ELENID
ELERI
ELWEN
ENIT
ERYL
FFION
GARWEN
GEINOR/GAENOR
GLAIN
GLENYE
GLENYS
GLYNWEN
GWALIA
GWANWEN
GWENDA
GWENDRAETH
GWENFOR
GWENLLIAN
GWENNAN

GWYLAN
ILAR
IONWEN
LILWEN
LLINOS
LLIO
MADRUN
MAELORWEN
MAI
MAIR
MAIRWEN
MANON
MARARED
MARCHELL
MARGED
MEDENI
MEDWEN
MELANGELL
MELERI
MENNA
MORGANT
MORVEN
MORWENA
MYFANWY
NERYS
NIA
NONA
NONNA
OLWEN
PRYDWEN
RHIAIA
RHIANNON
SANAN

SIANI
SIONED
SIWAN
TANGWEN
TEGAN

TELERI
TESI
TIRION
TYBIE

## B O Y S

AEDDAN
AERON
AFAN
ALAFON
ALAWN
ALDRYDD
ALDWYN
ALED
AMLYN
ANARAWD
ANEURIN
ARAWN
ARIAL
ARTHEN
ARWEL
AWSTIN
BAEDDAN
BARWYN
BEDO
BEDWYN
BEINON
BERIAN
BERWYN

BEUNO
BRADACH
BRENNIG
BROCHAN
BRWYNO
BRYCHAN
BRYN
BRYNACH
BRYNMOR
BRYS
CADAN
CADELL
CADFAEL
CADOG
CAERAU
CARADOG
CARWYN
CASWALLON
CEDWYN
CELLAN
CENNYDD
CERI
CIAN

CLYWD
COEL
COLLEN
COLWYN
CYBI
CYNAN
CYNFELYN
CYNGEN
DAFYDD
DEIAN
DEWI
DRYW
DUNAWD/DUNOD
DYBION
DYFAN
DYFED
EDERN
EIDIN
EIFION
ELAETH
ELIS
ELWYN
EMLYN
EMRYS
EMYR
EURION
GARWYN
GERAINT
GLYN
GOFANNON
GRUFFUDD
GUTO
GWENALLT

GWILYM
GWION
GWYDDON
GWYDION
GWYNEDD
GWYNFOR
GWYNORO
GWYR
HEW/HUW
HYWEL
IEUAN
IFAN
IFANWY
IFOR
IOLO
ISLWYN
IWAN
KYNAN
LLANDEN
LLELO
LLWYD
LLYN
LLYWELYN
MARLAIS
MEILYR
MEIRION
MERFYN
MEURYN
MIALL
MORFRAN
MORGANT
MORIEN
MYFYN

NINIAN
NISIEN
OSFAEL
OWAIN/OWEIN
PADARN
POWYS
RHAIN
RHEINALLT
RHODRI
RHUFON
RHUN
SAMLET
SEIRIOL
SEISYLL

SELWYN
SION
SULIEN
TALHAEARN
TALIESIN
TARAN
TATHAN
TEILO
TEYRNON
TRAHAEARN
TREFOR
TUDUR
TYSILIO
WYN

# INDEX

## GIRLS' NAMES

# INDEX

## BOYS' NAMES

# ABOUT THE AUTHORS

LINDA ROSENKRANTZ is the author of the novel *Talk* and co-author of *Gone Hollywood* and *SoHo*. The former editor of *Auction* magazine, she now writes a nationally syndicated column on collectibles. She currently lives in Los Angeles with her husband and daughter.

PAMELA REDMOND SATRAN, former fashion features editor of *Glamour*, writes a syndicated column aimed at working parents. Her freelance articles have appeared in numerous publications, including *Self*, *Elle*, *Working Mother*, and *The Washington Post*. She lives with her husband, daughter, and son in London.

Their first collaborative work, *Beyond Jennifer & Jason*, was so popular that it spawned a series of specialized naming books, which also includes *Beyond Sarah & Sam: An Enlightened Guide to Jewish Baby Naming* and *Beyond Shannon & Sean: An Enlightened Guide to Irish Baby Naming*.